T0209075

MY WAR

— IN THE —

JUNGLE

MY WAR
—➤ IN THE ◄—
JUNGLE

The Long-Delayed Memoir of a
Marine Lieutenant in Vietnam 1968–69

G. M. Davis

ARCHWAY
PUBLISHING

Archway Publishing books may be ordered through booksellers or by contacting:

Archway Publishing
1663 Liberty Drive
Bloomington, IN 47403
www.archwaypublishing.com
844-669-3957

ISBN: 978-1-6657-0081-8 (sc)
ISBN: 978-1-6657-0080-1 (hc)
ISBN: 978-1-6657-0082-5 (e)

Library of Congress Control Number: 2020925490

Print information available on the last page.

Archway Publishing rev. date: 02/26/2021

... He which hath no stomach to this fight,
Let him depart; his passport shall be made
And crowns for convoy put into his purse.
We would not die in that man's company
That fears his fellowship to die with us.
This day is called the feast of Crispian.
He that outlives this day, and comes safe home,
Will stand a-tiptoe when this day is named,
And rouse him at the name of Crispian.
He that shall live this day, and see old age,
Will yearly on the vigil feast his neighbors,
And say 'To-morrow is Saint Crispian.'
Then will he strip his sleeve and show his scars,
And say 'These wounds I had on Crispian's day'.

※ ※ ※

From this day to the ending of the world,
But we in it shall be remembered—
We few, we happy few, we band of brothers;
For he to-day that sheds his blood with me
Shall be my brother;
And gentlemen in England now-a-bed
Shall think themselves accursed they were not here,
And hold their manhoods cheap whiles any speaks
That fought with us upon Saint Crispin's day.

William Shakespeare, *Henry V*, Act 4, Scene III.

I started this memoir in part to honor those warriors who fought and sometimes fell alongside me in a conflict our nation would willingly forget. We must not let that happen; names on a wall are not enough. We who returned should ever stand a-tiptoe, strip our sleeves, and show our scars while others hold their manhoods cheap. We need not live or die in those men's company.

Dedication

This book is dedicated to the names on the Wall, and to the good and true Marines of Third Platoon, Kilo Company, Third Battalion, Ninth Marines, September 1968-March 1969.

Preface

This book began as ten or so typewritten pages many years ago. I wrote those pages trying to face a time I would sooner leave behind—to try to lay quiet the terrors of the past. A couple of old Marines I knew looked it over and told me to keep going. I have done so, in fits and starts, over the last fifteen years. It hasn't been easy. Vietnam veterans who read it now may also find it not easy. Still, writing about what happened fifty years ago has been cleansing to some degree.

Here I attempt to describe the action and the stillness, the aloneness and the camaraderie, the monotony and the excitement, the fear and the elation, the love and the hatred, and the overall misery involved in close combat. It was a time of life and death.

I have never thought that this story has been told—not my story necessarily, but the account of what it was like fighting toe-to-toe against a well-trained, well-supplied and well-motivated force in a jungle of almost impenetrable darkness. Hollywood and other authors of fiction and nonfiction have visited and revisited Vietnam over and over, but I don't think I have seen the war I fought either on the screen or in print. I believe the story, as I and the brave men who served with me experienced it, is worth telling.

And in the end, of course, a true war story is never about war. It's about sunlight. It's about the special way that dawn spreads out on a river when you know you must cross the river and march into the mountains and do things you are afraid to do. It's about love and memory. It's about sorrow. It's about sisters who never write back and people who never listen.

—Tim O'Brien, *The Things They Carried*

And while this is a memoir, it depends on the memory of things long past. If you see something you think is not factual, it is history to me. Personal war stories are invariably untrue, because the rush of adrenalin followed by the cleansing passage of time rewrites our own histories. Memories have no meaning. Who can say what really happened on any given day in close combat fifty years ago?

The names here are made up, but if you see yourself, I mean for it reflect positively, except for one person, about whom I simply present facts. Opinions are reserved for politicians.

Acknowledgments

First, I must thank my good friend Paul Reichs, a Marine lawyer I met in Okinawa during my convalescence. I decided to go to law school after Paul regaled me with his legal victories while we sat at the officers' club bar. He kept bugging me until I relented and started law school when I was released from active duty in September 1970. In school, I learned some law and ultimately thrived in a different kind of warfare—in the courtroom. Long ago, I sent a draft of an early manuscript of this project to Paul for his review. He passed it on to his wife, Kathy Reichs, who in turn did me the great honor of mentioning my manuscript in her 2010 book *Spider Bones*.

I owe a great debt of gratitude to a professional colleague, The Honorable Lacey Collier, Senior United States District Judge for the Northern District of Florida. Judge Collier is a Vietnam veteran who as a Naval Aviator flew 140 combat missions over North Vietnam, facing what was at the time the most sophisticated antiaircraft system operating anywhere in the world. He is one of my heroes. Judge Collier got wind of my project, read what I had written, and has been persistent in pushing me to publish it.

The manuscript was read at various points by several of my old Marine buddies, most of whom liked it, and none of whom discouraged my project, so their help is appreciated. I especially include a Marine I met in Okinawa, Pete Griffith, who didn't live to see the finished work thanks to the Agent Orange related cancer that took his life much too early. I miss you, Pete.

A psychologist friend, Dr. Paige Spencer, has helped read various sections of the book. She treats a lot of veterans from more recent wars and thinks this work will help her show other veterans suffering from PTSD that there can eventually be peace. I hope she is right.

Finally, I thank my wonderful wife, Linda, without whose encouragement I would have dropped the whole thing. I wrote what I wanted to write for myself. She said, like Dr. Spencer, that I should publish it for others.

− 1 −

The Kid

A few days into the 1969 Dewey Canyon operation, we were groping blind up another hill when the hell hammer struck.

"I'm hit!"

"Corpsman up! Second squad left, third squad right, on line, fire, and maneuver!" I shouted. I had shouted it many times. The men knew what to do, but I gave the order anyway.

We worked our way up the hill and spread out left and right, the jungle slowing progress to a crawl. I stayed on the trail and brought my following squad up behind me in reserve. It looked like we had run into a small killer team of NVA. The enemy usually defended his approaches with small suicidal units, but sometimes they would dig in an entire company and wait for us. Fire coming from the hilltop was not heavy, so this was likely a small team.

"Keep moving! Keep moving!" I went past the wounded point man, whose name I suddenly couldn't remember. "Hang in there, Marine!" I shouted.

He gave me a thumbs-up. Blood spurted from his leg like he had an artery wound, but Doc was with him.

"He'll make it, sir!" Doc yelled at my back.

I got to the crest of the hill. To my right, a Marine in third squad yelled, "Bunker!" and started firing into a hastily dug fighting hole covered with logs. The Marine next to him threw a grenade. His aim was perfect. Scratch one.

The shooting stopped as quickly as it had started. It turned out there were only two NVA here, and they were both dead. I saw the one in the bunker as he was blown apart. Before asking about the other one, I put the platoon in a defensive perimeter around a small clearing and called for medevac.

"Check out this gook, Mr. D," one of the men said. He pointed to the second corpse, a young North Vietnamese soldier, sitting in a fighting hole—shirtless. I wondered why he didn't have a shirt on. He wore regulation high-top shoes and green trousers. His green pith helmet, which provided no protection except from the sun and rain, was on the front edge of his fighting hole. A Chinese-made AK-47 lay across his lap.

He was motionless, leaning back against the side of his fighting hole. His eyes were open. He looked maybe seventeen, small, and well muscled with café au lait skin and jet-black hair. His slightly open mouth showed good teeth. A small hole just above his left nipple was his only visible wound. The freshly dug earth of his fighting hole absorbed the blood that had gushed from the exit wound in his back. Two minutes ago, he was the enemy doing what he could to kill Marines. Now he wouldn't be killing anyone. Now he was small and almost childlike.

Little came over and volunteered, "Fucked up his day, didn't we?"

I didn't respond. Something about this kid was disturbing. He was a dead NVA soldier, the enemy who wanted me dead. I had seen plenty of them. Usually, they were bloody and wore uniforms. They looked like soldiers. This kid did not look like a soldier. He didn't have a great grisly wound, and his blood was not easily visible. He looked like he was just sitting while holding his rifle. He looked like he was alive.

I stepped back and closed my eyes.

"You okay, Lieutenant?" asked Little.

"Yeah, fine."

I didn't want to look at this kid, but I couldn't stop myself. My mind wandered. The kid was somebody's son. He was somebody's husband or father maybe. Whoever had borne him, fed him, clothed him, nurtured him—whoever had loved and depended on him—would never know what happened to him. They would not know when or where or how he died, whether he fought bravely or died of some disease or accident. I guessed there would be no knock on the door by a casualty assistance officer. The kid would never return. The war would end, and he would not return. A life snuffed out.

He looked so young. I wondered who he was. A simple village farmer? A factory worker or student? It no longer mattered.

A sense of sorrow flitted through my head. More irony. He was the enemy, yet he knew and lived with the grit and grime, the filth and the privation, and the horror of very personal face-to-face combat. In the jungle, it was just him and me, and we were the same: hunters tracking our prey. He knew war like my Marines and I knew war. We had all lived it. He was one of us.

Identifying with the enemy is crazy, but those who have fought at the infantry level know that feeling, and only we can grasp it. I had seen it on TV: old World War II veterans drinking beer with former German soldiers, laughing about the adventure without reminding themselves of the deaths. Time had erased the worst of it. They had lived it too.

I felt a strange sense of cold squeezing in around me. A foggy mist seeped up and filled the air. My mind went off somewhere else. I felt what the kid had felt: the gut-wrenching fear that precedes a firefight.

> Americans were coming noisily up the hill. They were smelling of cigarettes and mosquito repellent, and their ammo cans were banging against weapons while they tried to be stealthy but failed beneath a hundred pounds of gear— and they were grunting with fatigue. I waited silently, my stomach in knots and chest so tight I could barely breathe. I could not see the Americans I heard because the jungle made them invisible.
>
> I started firing. Americans fired back. I never felt the random bullet impact into my chest. I had done what I had been trained to do, just as they had done. I was a soldier. I felt it all, and I was getting colder. The mist turned red, then black. I couldn't see. I was alone. I was dying. "Why me? I'm too young to die!" I would never go home. I was the kid.

"You sure you're okay, Lieutenant?" Little was insistent.

My mind and body jerked back to the present. "Yeah, fine. Just wondering about this kid."

"He's not a kid, sir, and what's to wonder about? He's a gook. He tried to kill us. He shot Robbins. Robbins may lose his leg, shot through the bone." Little seemed to suspect something.

"It was Robbins?" I asked, trying to deflect Little's questions. "I didn't get a good look as I went by him."

"Yes, sir."

"Robbins is a good man," I said. "I'm sure he'll be okay."

I turned and looked at Little. "Do you ever think of dying?"

Little blanched. "No, sir," he responded. "Not in this shithole anyway. I plan on living for a long time."

"Same here." That was all I could say.

Little grunted and went over to make sure Robbins was ready to be loaded on the approaching chopper. I was glad he went.

I couldn't let him sense my foreboding, if that's what it was. I needed someone to talk to, someone to tell me that I could wonder about this kid later, someone to tell me that shit happens and to get over it, someone to tell me that death is part of war, it happens to both sides, and to get over that too. But I was alone with the kid. There was no one else.

The helicopter arrived. Reality returned. I could still smell the greasy stench of blood and the acrid sting of gun smoke. And I could still sense fear. It was all around me. Anyone who says they were never afraid in the jungle is either a liar or insane—and likely both. Jungle combat is a relentless process in which the final product is either a live body or a dead one. Combat for the young man with the small hole in his chest was over. For the rest of us, combat was the present.

I told Corporal Gregg to have a couple of his men bury the kid.

He was incredulous. "Bury the gook, Mr. D? We were going to get some pictures with him."

"Bury him, Corporal. Cover him where he sits."

"Get your etools and cover this fucking gook," he told two of his Marines. And then he muttered something I'm glad I didn't quite catch. I knew he wondered just what the hell had come over his lieutenant. He would have to go on wondering. Any other dead enemy would have been left to the elements. I wouldn't have cared less if they posed with him for the folks at home.

These men understood that the fight was over but knew it wouldn't be the last. They had to prepare themselves mentally for the next. Americans in some unit sometime in the past had taken pictures of each other with an arm draped over a dead NVA or Vietcong, a cigarette in his lifeless mouth. There had also been reports of mutilations, including ears cut off. This had gotten to the press back home, and our Marines and soldiers were called cruel and inhumane. Taking a photograph with a dead enemy soldier was not kind, but it was not evil. It's hard to be either cruel or inhumane to a corpse, only disrespectful. These men were dead because they wanted us dead. Maybe in some college ethics class, you could make a dispassionate argument that we should respect our recently departed foe, but the jungle is not a dispassionate place. What the guys were doing was self-preservation. It was grasping at sanity in a world where sanity was slipping away into the jungle. They had survived another firefight. Disrespecting a dead enemy was a respite, however brief and however mean, until the next firefight and possibly the next dead Marine. No, my guys didn't cut the ears off corpses or otherwise desecrate them. They just mocked them.

But for whatever reason, I couldn't leave this kid to rot, so they buried him where he sat, refilling the fighting hole he had dug for his own protection. Now it would protect him forever. I buried my thoughts, putting off until some far-off time the reckoning I knew would come.

"All right, people, let's go. Third squad up. I'll follow third; first squad behind me and provide flank guards; second squad tail-end Charlie. Check your weapons and ammo, watch behind you, keep it slow, keep it quiet."

"Shit, Mr. D, the damn gooks know where we are," said Big Mike.

"Maybe, maybe not." I wouldn't affirm his fear, but the enemy knew we were coming, and I knew they were up there somewhere waiting for us.

As we saddled up, the remorse or compassion or whatever weak-kneed emotion that had been trying to engulf me disappeared. The surreal experience I had while standing over a dead NVA soldier was only a nightmare. I was back in the real world, and reality was limited only to whether we lived or died.

Anger and concentrated hatred returned. I hated them all, now more than ever. I wanted to kill them all, every goddamn one of them. I especially hated the now-buried kid in the hole who had joggled my conscience. At least I hadn't looked into his eyes before he died.

I moved my platoon up the hill. There would be more hills. There would be more death. Combat at the platoon level is a *danse macabre*, in which every man is waiting for some other poor bastard to get tapped on the shoulder. I could see no end to it.

I was getting too old for this shit. A week earlier, I had turned twenty-three.

— 2 —

This Was My War

My war against the North Vietnamese Army—the NVA—has lasted more than fifty years. I started this literary journey hoping to end it. Although the memories will never fade, most of the sharp and cutting fears I experienced then and carried home have largely quieted with time. But they haven't gone away.

I had the privilege of leading Marines. Marines were and are our national Spartans. For most of our country's history, Marines have been first to fight, have done more with less, have improvised and overcome, and have served with unswerving dedication. Marines personify undaunted determination and fearlessness. I believe I fit that mold, but my war, like all wars, was not fought on a sound stage, or in dress blues on a parade ground. It was fought in a hellish jungle where death hovered behind every tree and bush.

There, I learned that fearlessness does not mean unafraid. I was afraid to some degree every minute I was in the jungle and was terrorized in others. But fear does not mean cowardice. For an effective leader, it means overcoming the fear and acting with the competence needed at the moment. An old saying is that you can't be brave unless you are first afraid. That may or may not always be true, but I was brave when I needed to be.

Tolstoy said, "Happy families are all alike; every unhappy family is unhappy in its own way." My war was somewhere in between, so I try to describe it as it was—the good with the bad. Some truth is in all the Vietnam films, books, and articles that have come out over the years. A lot of it is crap. Either way, none have fully described what I saw.

I have forgotten some minor details over the years, but I remember and sometimes enter the mental cauldron of combat, and sense the emotional rupture of death and dismemberment, grope through the fog of war, and experience the fear and the elation and the loneliness of being there. Occasionally I remember the few precious good times.

My war was nothing more than the ordinary business of living and dying, of killing and being killed. For every man involved in infantry combat, war is a unique and very personal business. In the end, some live and some die. The dead ones are out of the war. The survivors never leave it.

Surviving combat means more than just staying alive.

— 3 —

Beer

The first night of my war was a good one. In the three or four days before that very pleasant evening I had endured an exhausting thirteen-hour flight from Los Angeles, with a short stop in Hawaii for fuel, to a day or two in Okinawa being issued combat uniforms and getting inoculated against who knows what, then another four hours flying from Okinawa to Vietnam with 164 other Marines on a Continental Airlines jet. We circled endlessly offshore from the Da Nang airbase, waiting for a landing slot between fighters and bombers taking off and landing. I wrote a postcard to my girlfriend: "Well, now that we all have sweaty palms and upset stomachs, let's get down and get on with it."

I was billeted for overnight processing in the Liberty City staff and officer barracks outside Da Nang, Republic of Vietnam. Liberty City was perfectly named if you were being processed out for return home. A couple of second-tour staff sergeants who had been on my flight suggested we go for a beer. We were in a war zone, and going out for a beer seemed like a strange idea, and I was physically beat, but I was up for something that might keep my mind off the reality of where I was and what I would be doing for the next year.

We went across what passed for the street—a dirt road—to the Navy Construction Battalion compound. The Seabees build things, including their own compounds. When a Seabee battalion rotates home, it must by custom leave the compound in better shape than when it arrived. In a world that seemed to be nothing but dirt and heat and dust and more heat, a succession of worker bees had built themselves a resort. I didn't take the tour. The beer beckoned.

The staff and officers' club was in a bunker, a twenty-by-twenty-foot reinforced wood building covered with sandbags. Opening the door was like going home to a favorite neighborhood bar—a real bar, with low lighting, air conditioning, neon beer signs, Schlitz beer coasters, a jukebox, and cold beer. Real cold beer. Lots of real cold beer, a dime a glass, no limit. I thought I must have died already. For me, the war was only a few days in the future, but it was far away from a bar across the street from Liberty City.

"If this is the way to fight a war," I said. "I'm all for it." My companions laughed.

"Lieutenant," one said, "it won't be like this out there."

"Out there" in the jungle, there were only Marines and the enemy, and the rules of engagement were simple: If he isn't Marine, kill him.

I knew that. My MOS—military occupational specialty—was 0301, basic (meaning trained but inexperienced) infantry officer. I soon became a rifle platoon leader in Kilo Company,

Third Battalion, Ninth Marine Regiment. During the seven months I was in Vietnam, I never again experienced a night like the one in the bar at the Seabee compound.

In the Vietnam movies we have seen over the years, the troops are always drinking, smoking pot, burning villages, screwing the local whores, whatever. I didn't see or do any of that. In the jungle, I never saw a woman, Vietnamese or otherwise, not even a nurse. Beer was a rare commodity in the jungle. Even on the few occasions when the resupply helicopters brought us beer, it was warm. I ate C-rations (Meal Combat Individual), which are worse than the MREs of today's military, which are not particularly good either. I never saw anyone smoking pot. I never set foot in a Vietnamese village or burned one either.

Where I fought, there were no USO shows, no Bob Hope or Led Zeppelin, no dignitaries or celebrities, no China Beach, no bars, no cots, much less clean sheets, and no way to feel reasonably safe. There was simply no relief from war. I sometimes wonder if the entertainers who generously gave of their time ever knew that we, the ones doing the real dirty work, never saw them, never even knew they were there. Our isolation may be hard to believe based on all the fantasy— mostly crap—movies produced over the years, but my war was not on the populated coast against the Viet Cong, it was in the jungle against the NVA.

The Viet Cong were deadly, no question, and elusive, hiding among the civilian populace. They generally avoided direct combat, preferring to blow off a Marine's legs with a booby trap, much like the IED's in Iraq and Afghanistan—the wars of the next generation. The North Vietnamese Army, on the other hand, was a well-trained, well-equipped, and motivated professional army that didn't shrink from a fight. I am still not sure which was worse.

Sitting in an air-conditioned bar at a Seabee compound just outside Da Nang drinking cold beer, I hadn't yet experienced any of that. I wrote "First night in Vietnam" on a Schlitz coaster and put it in my pocket. I was twenty-two years old.

— 4 —

Boots

Next morning, in mid-September 1968, I hitched a ride on a CH-46 helicopter headed to Third Marine Division headquarters at Dong Ha, Republic of Vietnam. I had arrived the day before from what I soon learned was universally referred to as "The World"—home.

I ran up the chopper's rear hatch, dumped my seabag on the deck, and sat on a bench near the after hatch. The CH-46 has an engine with a rotor at each end with what loosely qualifies as a cabin between, with long canvas or nylon benches flanking each side. Nothing is made for comfort, and nothing is hidden from view. All the helicopter's wires, hoses, fuel lines, and everything that would otherwise be behind the wall in a civilian aircraft are visible. Staring at all this complexity always made me a little nervous about flying in helicopters.

At first, I thought I was the only passenger on board, but I soon realized someone else was traveling with me. Toward the front of the cabin, a pair of boots stuck out from under a poncho. The boots were worn and dusty, the black dye of the leather long since worn away to buckskin. I later learned that it took a few months for the jungle vegetation or, in open areas, the elephant grass, to scrape the dye off a pair of boots. If you had black leather on your boots, you were an FNG—a fucking new guy—and you knew nothing. If your boots were buckskins, you were a veteran.

The poncho shrouded a body lying on a stretcher. The stretcher and the body and the poncho and the boots were on the deck of the helicopter. The boots were dancing, moving in time to the whop-whop-whop of the rotors. The rest of the stretcher showed no sign of life. There were only dancing boots, laced to a corpse.

My boots were black. I had been a Marine for almost exactly a year, had been in country for less than twenty-four hours, and was looking at boots on a dead Marine. I wanted to look at something else, to think about something else, but I was alone with the noise and the vibration and the boots. I wondered how this Marine had died. I hoped that it was quick and painless and that he never saw it coming. I would never know. I would never know who he was, or his age, or his rank, or his unit. When the helicopter landed after a thirty-minute flight, someone would carry him off to the division morgue. He would then go back to Da Nang and ultimately home.

The only dead people I had ever seen were my grandparents, who had benefitted from the mortician's magic to make them look alive before being placed in silk-lined caskets. All I could see of this Marine were his boots. I thought about his parents, his wife or girlfriend. They were back in The World, going about their business, oblivious to their imminent grief. They didn't know the awful reality that I knew. It would hit them when a Marine officer in dress blues knocked on their door and asked to come in. I wouldn't want to be there.

I wondered how long it would be before I saw more dead men, not wrapped in ponchos, but laying on the ground, up close. Probably not long. And me? It was accepted dogma, whether it was true or not, that Marine lieutenants didn't last long in the bush. I wasn't afraid of dying, although the boots had a sobering effect. If I was afraid of anything, it was of screwing up.

I had survived the rigorous training of Officers Candidate School and the Basic School, and I knew I was a leader. I was a Marine infantry officer who would soon take over a rifle platoon and be entrusted with the lives of forty to fifty young men. The exact number of my men changed constantly, almost daily, always determined by casualties, sick call, R&R, and rotations home. My job—the job of every Marine—would be to accomplish the mission, which in this war meant to kill the enemy and keep my men alive.

Training had taught me that killing the enemy would be the simpler part; my platoon of Marines would be my weapon. I had few doubts about my abilities, but I understood the problem of needless deaths caused by inept leadership, the universal curse of the foot soldier—an affliction as old as warfare.

I had been to school, but school is not combat. Back in The World a leader could study reports, listen to advisers, and make what hopefully was the right decision. A combat leader does not have reports, advisers, or the "hopefully" option. He must be right under pressure, and he must be right in a hurry.

To me, being an inept leader causing needless deaths would be worse than dying. In combat, performance at the platoon level is graded only in life and death; the results are written in blood, not ink.

I had to relax. I was where I was. I had volunteered, and I was getting on with it, but I could not ignore the boots. They seemed alive even though it was obvious they were just boots on a dead Marine wrapped in a poncho laying on a stretcher in a helicopter, doing their macabre dance. It was starkly impersonal, it was disturbing, and it was war. Hopefully, it was not a harbinger. Either way, the war would come to me soon enough.

— 5 —

The Place

Vietnam clings to Laos and Cambodia (now Kampuchea) on the eastern side of Indochina like a twelve-hundred-mile-long legless dragon. The Annamite Range forms its spine. The dragon's head is in the north, where its curious mouth seems to be devouring a chunk of Laos. Its tail wraps to the south and west and ends against southern Cambodia at the Mekong River delta. Quang Tri Province is at about its center, measuring about sixty miles wide, extending from the sea to the Laotian border. My war played out there, along the dragon's spine just below the DMZ—the demilitarized zone—a no-man's land that was not demilitarized in any sense.

Before the Second World War, activists in the northern part of Vietnam, led by Ho Chi Minh, formed a communist party to oppose the occupying French. They called their organization the Viet Minh, roughly translated League for the Independence of Vietnam. Over time the Viet Minh became an armed force of guerrillas operating against the French and later against the Japanese. After the Japanese were ousted at the end of World War II, the French returned, and the Viet Minh continued their struggle in what came to be known as the First Indochina War. In 1954 the French effectively lost the war at Dien Bien Phu. The resulting Geneva Accord left Vietnam divided into the communist North and the democratic South. Soon, communists in South Vietnam organized a guerrilla army, the Viet Cong, or National Liberation Front.

In the late 1950s and early 1960s the United States, buying into and fearing the domino theory of successive communist takeovers in Southeast Asia, started sending military supplies and then advisers to assist the South Vietnamese Army. The Viet Cong gained strength with the help of the North Vietnamese, who were, in turn, supported and supplied by the Soviet Union and China. Neither side was backing down, and the conflict escalated.

Major Dale Buis and Master Sergeant Chester Ovnand, serving as advisers to the South Vietnamese army, were killed by Viet Cong guerillas on July 8, 1959. Their names are first and second on the Vietnam Veterans Memorial Wall in Washington, DC. The first American killed in Vietnam was Technical Sergeant Richard Fitzgibbon, who was murdered by another American serviceman on June 8,1956. His name was added to the Wall in 1999.

In August 1964 the destroyer USS *Maddox*, showing the flag in the Gulf of Tonkin near North Vietnam, was gathering electronic intelligence when it engaged three North Vietnamese torpedo boats. Who fired first is disputed. Also disputed is the existence of a second attack on *Maddox* two days later. Responding to these questionable outrages, Congress passed the Gulf of Tonkin Resolution, effectively ceding its constitutional war power to the president, a power, incidentally, it has never reclaimed. The Marines landed at Da Nang, in the northern part of South Vietnam, led by my future regiment, the Ninth Marines, in March 1965.

The borders between South Vietnam and its neutral neighbors, Laos and Cambodia, were and are just lines on a map in a trackless jungle running along the spine of the Annamite Mountains. The mountains are old and worn, most reaching to no more than three thousand feet. You could not escape the jungle by climbing to the top of a mountain; it was everywhere in the western part of the country. At the international borders, there were no roads, no walls or fences or barbed wire, and certainly no border guards standing by little guard shacks operating barber-pole gates. There was only jungle.

The Marines fought regular North Vietnamese Army units in the mountainous jungle, yet they could not follow when the enemy retreated to their sanctuaries in Laos and Cambodia. The North Vietnamese operated in those countries and the demilitarized zone with impunity. Neither Laos nor Cambodia had an effective army. They were powerless to eject the North Vietnamese even if they were so inclined.

We were not allowed to follow the enemy when they retreated across borders. Our country's supposed moral superiority in refusing to violate the fictional neutrality of these places was insane. The NVA had safe places to rest and regroup their troops and had a supply line, the Ho Chi Minh Trail, impervious to interdiction except by air. Air attacks had some effect, but never closed the trail. Not allowing ground troops to follow the NVA into its sanctuaries arguably gave us some legitimacy on the international stage, but it was a military disaster. It is now clear that we were fighting a war we could not possibly win. I did not appreciate that rather important fact in 1968. As I will show later, our political leaders knew it well but sacrificed fifty-eight thousand American lives anyway.

– 6 –

The FNG

So, on day one, I drank beer. On day two, I flew with the boots and their dead Marine, then reported to the company rear in Dong Ha where the clerks and admin people were and drew my gear. The company first sergeant told me matter-of-factly that Kilo Company had been in a pretty vicious firefight a week before and that I would take the place of a lieutenant who had gone down. I detected on him a slight smirk that was less than reassuring. The first sergeant was staying in the rear to run the administrative part of Kilo's war. I was going to the jungle.

At the supply shack, I picked up my "782 gear:" jungle boots, socks, jungle utility uniform, backpack, flak jacket, helmet, pistol, several loaded magazines, and first aid kit. Everything I needed.

"And there you go, Lieutenant, two canteens." The supply sergeant eyed me with smug assurance as if he knew what my response would be.

"Two? That's it?"

"That's all I can give you." We locked eyes for a second before he looked down. "Don't worry, sir, you'll have all you need."

I thought about the dead Marine I had seen on the chopper when I flew up from Da Nang that morning. His body was wrapped in a poncho. All his gear lay beside him on the deck, but there were no canteens. I nodded to the supply sergeant. "Got it," I said.

"Good luck, sir," he responded. I knew he wasn't wishing me luck in acquiring more canteens.

On day three I took command of my platoon on a hilltop called Fire Support Base Henderson, a mile or so northwest of the famous Rockpile—an eight-hundred-foot mountain that stood above the surrounding terrain and looked like a large pile of rocks—in the northernmost province of South Vietnam, less than a mile south of the DMZ. From day three until I went back to Okinawa seven months later, I was at the company rear exactly twice, and I spent the night there once, in the hospital recovering from a gunshot wound. My entire tour was in the bush, the mountainous jungle, or, for brief respites, at a primitive muddy forward area called Vandegrift Combat Base (VCB), which was reasonably safe, but was not "the rear."

A chopper dropped me off on a primitive landing zone (LZ) at Fire Support Base Henderson, where I was to join Kilo Company and take command of my platoon. When the chopper lifted off, I was left standing in the middle of the LZ wearing my new black boots with green mesh insets, and my new green utility uniform and flak jacket with my new pack on my back. My new holster contained a reasonably new

Model 1911A1 .45 caliber semiautomatic pistol, and my two green plastic canteens in new canvas canteen holders were attached to my new web belt. The holster's leather creaked. I don't think anybody ever looked more like a fucking new guy than I did at that moment.

The LZ was at the highest point of Hill 725, measured in meters, about twenty-four hundred feet above sea level, and I was looking at a foreign world. The remains of trees lay around the LZ's perimeter. Combat engineers used C-4 explosives to blast them down and create a clearing for helicopters. The trees were splayed outward as though a bomb had gone off in the center of the LZ.

I saw a lot of Marines in various stages of dress. Some were shirtless, some wore green T-shirts, and some wore their uniform shirts. Their uniforms looked ragged and dirty. *They definitely would not pass inspection back in The World*, I thought, which was a stupid thing to think.

It was hot. All the Marines I could see were either sitting or lying down. Their faces and as much of the rest of their bodies as I could see were dirty as if mud had dried on them, which was probably the case. On the other hand, there was no trash lying around. The thin, black, pungent smoke wafting across the LZ from the north told me someone was burning trash. I smelled cigarette smoke and DEET, two odors that have never gone away. It didn't look like anybody was on watch.

I heard a tiny zing and swatted a mosquito as it landed on my face. There was no noise other than the low murmur of men talking. The silence was disturbing. This was the jungle, yet the hoots and caws from the old Tarzan movies were missing.

Hooches of varying description lay in an arc about thirty meters down the hill. The hooches were made by snapping two poncho liners together. Most of them were draped over a pole of some sort. A California state flag on a small surviving tree flew next to one of the hooches. Everything was covered in dust.

Beyond my immediate surroundings to the north, a chain of mountains hid the DMZ. Behind me, to the south, the lazy brown line of Highway 9 passed east and west along the base of more mountains. On my left, the jungle hid what was behind it. On my right, a path led down to another LZ. The South China Sea was visible on the horizon, twenty or so miles to the east.

No welcoming committee appeared. Not wanting to look stupid by just standing there, I walked over to the edge of the LZ where I had seen the path. A lot of Marines were lounging around the fallen trees, but none looked up as I passed. They looked busy doing nothing in particular, and nobody said anything. The path I had seen led down about fifty meters to a cleared area where howitzers were located. I figured the company headquarters would be there.

At the bottom of the hill, I stopped a Marine. I had no idea who he was, or his rank, or why he was shirtless and wearing utility trousers cut off at the knees.

"Where is your Skipper, Marine?" I asked.

Eying the shiny gold second lieutenant's bars on my collars, he grinned and nodded toward a Marine standing not far off.

"That's him, the one with the notebook." He turned, spit, and walked away.

At least the one with the notebook has his shirt on, I thought. I walked over to him, saluted smartly, and reported: "Lieutenant Davis reporting as ordered, sir."

He didn't return my salute.

"We don't salute in the jungle, Lieutenant. Our friends out there like to kill officers, and you just told any enemy who might be watching that I'm a good target."

I lowered my hand slowly.

"Yes, sir. Sorry, sir."

He eyed me like I was a creature from outer space, dropped without warning into his artillery battery.

"I'm the CO of this battery," he said dryly, "and I'm not expecting any new second lieutenants. You probably belong to the infantry, so your company commander is somewhere back up the hill you just came down. I suggest you go back up and find him."

"Yes, sir." *Dear God, if there were ever an FNG contest, I would win the grand prize.*

I headed back up the hill. About halfway up a guy lounging on the ground with some other Marines held out his hand.

"Bill," he said, "Bill Michaelson. I'm your company commander. I see you met my counterpart with the artillery." Michaelson's pronounced Brooklyn accent sounded out of place, but then why not Brooklyn? This was America's Marine Corps.

I shook his hand. He was wearing the standard utility uniform, but I didn't see any rank insignia. He was about five feet ten and looked old—not ancient old, but a lot older than the typical twenty-four or twenty-five-year-old captain.

"Yes, sir."

"Call me Bill, not sir," he said.

"Yes, ... um, okay, Bill."

He looked me up and down and said, "We need to talk." He got up and walked me over to a clear area where there were no men within earshot.

"It's Davis, right? They told us you were coming."

"That's me."

"Okay, look, I'm a first lieutenant. Lieutenants, second or first, do not 'sir' each other. And I saw you being taught not to salute anybody in the jungle."

I started to relax a little.

"You could say."

"Captain Siler's okay for an arty guy, so don't let it bother you. They shoot their guns in support of our operations. Right now, we, meaning Kilo Company, are providing security for his battery. The rest of the battalion is out in the jungle around here looking for NVA. A week ago, we had a pretty good scrap, so we're getting a little break."

Standing guard around a fixed position sounded ideal to give me time to get to know my men and get snapped in on the routine.

"Sounds good," I said.

He laughed and slapped me on the shoulder. "Don't get used to it." I learned later that Michaelson was a Mustang, a former enlisted man, an E-9 sergeant major, I think. He had been commissioned for limited duty when the Marines needed experienced men to command rifle companies and was short of captains, primarily due to casualties. It happens in wartime.

"C'mon. I'll take you to meet your NCOs."

NCOs, noncommissioned officers, Marines who have proven leadership qualities, are the corporals and above who form the backbone of the Corps. My NCOs included my squad leaders, the men in charge of the guts of my platoon.

We walked on up the hill to the LZ where I had started. Where's Little?" Michaelson asked.

A gravelly, very southern voice from the other side of the LZ announced: "I'm over here, Skipper."

Staff Sergeant Little, who would be my platoon sergeant and strong right hand for the next seven months, walked over and shook my hand. He was average in height, tanned, and well built without looking like a jock. He wore no rank insignia that I could see. His boots were buckskins. He wore standard, very faded formerly olive-green utility trousers and a Marine Corps green sweatshirt with the sleeves cut off. It read "MARINES" across the front. I never saw him wear any other shirt, hot or cold, rain or shine.

"Glad you're here, Lieutenant. That means you got the platoon now, and I can relax."

Michaelson laughed. "Don't believe him. Little is one of the best NCOs in the company. You are lucky to have him. He will teach you everything you need to know, won't you Little?"

Little nodded slightly. "Aye, sir."

The Skipper started back toward his area, then turned his head.

"The platoon leaders will be meeting at my hooch at 1600. Be there. And take your bars off. They love to kill officers."

"Will do, sir, uh … Bill, uh … Skipper."

I looked back at Little, who was staring at me. I couldn't read his reaction, but I'm sure he thought I was the idiot I felt.

"Take your bars off and pin one on the inside of your collar, sir," Little volunteered. "Some officers wear them on the flaps of the grenade pouches on their trousers. Out here you won't need them anyway. We'll know who you are."

Yeah, I thought, *the greenhorn lieutenant in the new green suit.* I took the bars off and put one on my grenade pocket flap.

"I got your squad leaders together when you landed," he said. "I tried to get your attention, but you walked off the other side of the LZ."

I nodded. He had probably gone over and witnessed the disaster with Captain Siler, but he never mentioned it.

He motioned across the LZ. "Over there."

Six Marines were seated on the ground in a rough circle. They stood up as I approached, and we all shook hands. I took off my pack and motioned for everyone to sit.

In 1968, a Marine rifle platoon was made up of three rifle squads of thirteen men each, plus attached machine guns and rockets. Each squad had a squad leader, a sergeant. The squad was subdivided into three fire teams of four men, one of whom was a corporal fire team leader. That, at least, was according to the TO, the table of organization, but we never had all the sergeants and corporals the TO allowed us thanks to casualties and rotations home. I guessed it had to do mostly with casualties.

Staff Sergeant Little was the senior enlisted man. He introduced the others. Sergeant Manning was the platoon guide. The guide acts as the admin chief and assistant platoon sergeant. Manning was a short, skinny guy who looked older than his age. He also looked like he belonged in the pay office, not the infantry. Looks are deceiving, though. I saw soon enough that he was one hell of a grunt Marine.

My three rifle squad leaders were Sergeant Williams, who was African American, Corporal Gregg, who was a Canadian, and Corporal McFarland, another Black guy who hailed from somewhere in Florida.

A Marine rifle company has three rifle platoons and a weapons platoon. The Skipper had parceled out the machine guns and the rockets from the weapons platoon to his three rifle platoons. The rest of the weapons platoon, the M-60 mortars, stayed with the company command section.

My machine-gun section leader was Corporal Sessions, a red-headed, freckled kid who would have been a perfect Opie when he was younger. Lance Corporal Jones, another Black Marine, was rocket team leader. I noted that he sported a very short afro, which was a little long for a Marine, but I would worry about that later. The rocket team carried 40 mm LAAWs, Light Antitank Assault Weapons. They looked like a miniature version of the old bazookas of World War II. Supposedly LAAW's were good against tanks. It didn't take a genius to figure out that there were no tanks in the mountainous jungle. I asked Little what the LAAWs were used for.

"Clearing caves. We find them sometimes. If there are any gooks in them, we seal them in with rockets." He grinned. "Sometimes we just 'think' there's gooks in a cave, so we bust them too. It gives the men practice."

Sessions and Jones nodded enthusiastically.

With the introductions over, I wasn't sure how to proceed, so I launched into the opening spiel I had outlined in my head the day before.

"Gentleman, you can see that I'm new. I don't deny it. I don't claim to know anything about what you've been doing out here, but I'm ready to learn and lead at the same time. Staff Sergeant Little will be my teacher. I'm told he's the best. I'm a fast learner."

Silence. My oratory skills were not impressive.

"All right, you men return to your areas. I'll be around later to meet your guys and check out our position."

They got up and wandered off without saying anything. I noticed that Jones had used a black marker to print "Nguvu Za Weusi" in large letters on the back of his flak jacket. I had no idea what that meant. I would deal with it later.

I turned to Little.

He shrugged. "You'll do fine, sir. The only thing we were afraid of was getting a know-it-all. We all know you're new at this, but you'll be a veteran after our first firefight. You won't be the first new lieutenant many of these men have seen. It don't take long to get adjusted."

"So, what's the first thing I need to know?" I asked.

"Rely on me and your squad leaders. They're all good men. We've been through some bad shit together, and we've lost some men. It happens. Like all Marines, we rely on each other."

I thought of the lieutenant I was replacing. Little could read my thoughts. "We lost our lieutenant a few days back. It was just bad luck. Shit happens. Your squad leaders are the best."

"What are their weaknesses?"

"I guess the thing nobody does worth a damn is read a map. The maps we get are old. Maybe the French made the originals, who knows? But the jungle is so thick you can't see anything but what's right in front of you. I hope you're good at it, sir, because we have to know where we are."

I understood. I almost told him that I got perfect marks at the Basic School in mapping and terrain appreciation and that I could read a map with the best of them but thought better. Better to prove it than to brag it. "So, if we have to call in artillery or close air support, we want it on the enemy and not on us."

"Fuckin' A, sir."

My eyes narrowed; I didn't get that one. Little could tell I wasn't snapped in on the lingo yet.

"It's a term everybody uses, at least the enlisted guys do. It means 'affirmative.' It's not disrespectful. They won't use it around you until they're comfortable with you. When they do, you'll know they trust you."

I wasn't sure what that meant, but I wasn't going to embarrass myself further.

"It's nearly 1600," I said. "I've got to go meet with the Skipper. Why don't you come along?"

"Roger that."

Little and I walked back across the LZ. I asked if he knew what was up. He didn't.

"Does the Skipper have a conference every day?" I asked.

"No, sir. The first one for me."

When we got to the company command post, the two other platoon leaders were there. Second Lieutenant Bill Washburn commanded first platoon. Second Lieutenant Steve Roberts commanded second. They welcomed me and acknowledged Little.

Washburn said, "Looks like you're off the hook now, Little."

"Can't say I'm sorry."

The Skipper raised his hand. "Take notes, gentlemen."

Luckily, I had a pen and notebook in my breast pocket. Not having them would have been the perfect final disaster for a day filled with stupidity.

The Skipper started without notes: "We are being relieved

here tomorrow. We are going to Camp Carroll, where we will stand lines until further orders. There is no reported enemy activity in the area, but the company that has been providing security at Carroll is going out for a night envelopment of a nearby village. Don't know where. The artillery here will begin lifting out from here at 0600. They expect to be gone in two hours, and we will lift out beginning at 0800, give or take."

Damn, I just got here, and we're already leaving, I thought, *and where is Camp Carroll?*

"We will go in order of first platoon, followed by the company command and mortars, second platoon, with third platoon last. Lieutenant Davis, your people will be the last ones off the hill. The hill is being abandoned for now so make sure your people are on watch until the last flight out. We'll get noon chow at Carroll. We will be on our usual radio frequencies. Davis, make sure your radio has the flyboy freqs since you'll be talking to them."

"Got it, Skipper."

"When we get to Carroll, I'll assign each platoon an area. You gentlemen can set your lines then. Any questions, I'm here until I'm there."

I'll be damned. All through the Basic School, they drilled us with their famous five-paragraph order, which we would be expected to issue to our troops. It had an acronym, like everything else in the military, SMEAC. And now I had heard one off the cuff.

Situation: We're leaving here and closing the Fire Support Base.

Mission: We will stand lines at Camp Carroll. No enemy expected.

Execution: Choppers at 0800. Platoons in order, CP to follow first platoon.

Admin and Logistics: Chow at Carroll followed by relieving other company in place.

Command and communications: Get your frequencies, ask me if any questions.

In training, this stuff got drilled into our heads as if it was the most important thing in the world, to the point that we began to sweat being able to issue a five-paragraph order. The Skipper did it without notes. SMEAC. Ha. Somehow it gave me some assurance that all this bureaucratic crap they beat into us had a practical end.

Little and I walked back to the third platoon area.

"Our platoon corpsman, 'Doc,'" said Little, "is on R&R. He should be back tomorrow. The Skipper has the senior doc with him if we need anything."

A Marine got a week of rest and recuperation after about six months in country. The most popular destinations were Australia, Kuala Lumpur, Bangkok, Hong Kong, Hawaii, and Singapore. Most of the married guys went to Hawaii to spend a week with their wives. The overwhelming choice in my platoon was Singapore, where the whores were beautiful, numerous, and cheap, or so they told me.

More than one of my men returned from Singapore desperately in love with his lady, who, like Julia Roberts in *Pretty Woman*, wasn't really a whore but needed money to go to college, or to support an invalid parent, or something. The men swore that after getting back to The World they would go back and rescue their maiden. I always wondered if any did. I would bet that if they tried, they were disappointed.

The week of R&R usually ended up being two weeks

away from the platoon because of travel time and medical care. A Marine returning from R&R was usually kept in the rear for a few days for treatment for STDs, in those days called venereal disease, whether he needed it or not.

"I hope they don't drop Doc off here when everybody's gone," I said, stupidly.

"Hadn't thought of that," said Little. He pursed his lips for a few seconds like he was working on a solution. Then, "They'll figure it out."

I didn't know how they would figure out whatever needed to be figured out, but I was sure the helo guys were not going to land on a vacant and undefended LZ.

"Does Doc have a name?" I asked.

"Crozier. Don't know his first name. We call him Doc."

As we approached our platoon CP, a large man unbent himself from a squatting position and stood up. When he finally reached his full height, he was well over six feet tall. I never was sure exactly how tall he was. The muscles in his tanned biceps and forearms rippled like waves on the ocean. Big waves. His baby face stood out more than his size, though.

"Lieutenant Davis," Little said, "this is Lance Corporal Whelan. He's known as Big Mike."

No surprise on the nickname. We shook hands. He could have crushed mine.

"Lance Corporal Whelan," I said, as I shook his hand. They had taught us not to be too informal around our men, so I didn't use the nickname. That came later.

"Mike's an 0621," Little continued. "He'll be your radioman." I didn't know what an 0621 was but wasn't surprised to learn it was a field radio operator. All I knew were the 03xx military occupational specialties—infantry.

Whelan had been cleaning dust and mud off his radio as Little and I approached. The radio was a standard PRC-25. It weighed more than twenty pounds. As I would soon learn, Whelan carried the radio on top of his backpack. He also carried an M-16 rifle with eight or ten loaded magazines, five or six canteens, each holding a quart of water, spare C-ration cans, extra socks, letter writing gear tightly wrapped in plastic, and any other personal items he felt he could carry. The standard Marine pack did not hold much, but Whelan carried quite a load. I wondered if they considered the size and strength of a man when they assigned him to communications.

I turned to Little. "Tell me how all this works at night. Who does what and when?"

"You mean with the radio?"

"Yeah."

Little rubbed the stubble on his chin. It looked like he hadn't shaved in a couple of days. "The platoon leader and his radioman always hooch together, but that's your choice. Mike is pretty good at putting up a decent hooch. We stand radio watch at night, two hours each, Mike, me, Doc, and Sergeant Manning. You can take a turn if you want."

I would have to think about that.

"For the time being," I said, "wake me every time there's a shift change. I'll check the lines then."

Little nodded. I honestly didn't know what the protocol, if you can call it that, was. I would talk to the other platoon leaders. There were a lot of simple things they hadn't taught us in the Basic School.

I asked Little to show me our sector of the perimeter. "It will be dark fairly soon, and I want to meet the men in the platoon."

"This way," he said. "We'll start on the right end where we tie in with second platoon and end up at the left and where we tie in with first platoon."

I spent the next hour meeting my troops. They were all respectful, even friendly. I would get to know them all personally in due course. For now, it was a name and a handshake. Some were cleaning their weapons, and some were writing letters or reading a paperback book. Many had been asleep. I satisfied myself that at least one man every twenty-five meters or so was watching the jungle. The enemy usually attacked before dawn or at dusk and sometimes in complete darkness. They rarely attacked a fixed position during daylight, but I wasn't taking chances.

The men divided into two-man teams within their own squad. Each pair would dig a fighting hole for their sector, then set up a hooch behind it where they would take turns sleeping on the ground. Every fighting hole had a cleared field of fire in front. Some, depending on the terrain and the size of the trees, extended out only a few meters. Where they could, they might be able to clear enough vegetation to extend their field of fire out fifty meters.

They would also set out trip flares, wired at ankle height across their entire sector. If there was a ground attack, the trip flares would light up before the enemy got too close. That was the idea anyway.

As I saw each squad leader and team leader, I told them we would be lifting out at 0800 the next day and to be at my hooch at 0730 for further instructions. When the introductions were done, I went back to the hooch I would now share with Whelan. We chatted about nothing in particular as we ate our C-ration meal. When dusk began to settle on our hilltop, the platoon stood to, meaning every man was awake, standing in his fighting hole, with his weapon pointed out. When it was fully dark, and the enemy hadn't shown himself, we stood down. When we stood down, I walked the platoon's sector with Whelan and his radio behind me, to make sure someone was awake in each fighting hole. Then we returned to our hooch.

I hadn't done anything all day, but I was exhausted. Probably mentally more than physically, but I was worn out. It was good to get my boots off, even for a couple of hours. Whelan unzipped his boots, something I wasn't prepared for. He had laced a zipper down the front of each boot. When he pulled the zipper down the boot flared as if it were completely untied and loosened and was easy to get on and off.

"Where'd you get the zipper?" I asked. "That's pretty clever."

"They're available back in the rear, sir," he replied. "The people make them in the villages and sell them. I paid two bucks for mine."

I sat there for a moment without saying anything. I knew enough to understand that in the jungle we would sleep in hastily erected hooches for a couple of nights and then move on. Taking our boots off at night would be necessary. I didn't know if the trench foot our grandfathers suffered from in the First World War had a modern equivalent, but having constantly wet feet couldn't be healthy.

The obvious downside of taking your boots off at night is looping and tying old cotton laces to get them back on quickly if attacked. It frustrated me to think that while our government provided us with the best equipment of any armed force in the world, it took some Vietnamese dress maker to come up with the idea of using zippers to get boots on and off quickly.

"Does everyone in the platoon have them?" I asked.

"No, sir," he replied. "Some do, but not many. We just recently found out about them. I was in the rear for a couple of days two weeks ago and got mine."

Damn, I thought. I was in the rear for a day and none of the REMFs, the rear echelon motherfuckers, said anything about two-dollar zippers for boots. But then they didn't need them. They slept secure in tent-covered wooden huts.

"Did you get the aviation frequencies for tomorrow, Whelan?"

"Yes, sir.

"Do you know where Camp Carroll is?"

"Somewhere back toward the coast, but I'm not sure."

"So, do you know what's there, what kind of base it is?"

"No, sir."

I should kick myself. I'm the officer who is supposed to know things, yet here I am pumping a lance corporal for information.

"You can probably get some boot zippers there, though," he volunteered.

"Yeah. I hope so."

Once it's fully dark in the jungle, there's nothing to do. No lights are allowed. No one talks above a whisper. Night vision would be possible in the next war, but not this one, where the enemy owned the night.

Whelan had the first two hours of radio watch, so I went to sleep on the ground. I had a "Snoopy blanket" for cover—actually, a poncho liner measuring six feet by six feet, made of a quilted synthetic material patterned in camouflage. The Snoopy was very light but kept us warm even in the rain on a cold night. How they got their nickname, I never knew. I always figured somebody conflated Snoopy with Linus, who always carried a blanket, and the name stuck. I was pondering that mystery as I drifted off to sleep.

During my first night on the ground, I discovered that my fond childhood memories of camping out had been misleading. Sleeping on the bare ground while listening to the watch make periodic security checks with the listening posts outside the perimeter, and then being awakened every two hours and getting up to put on my boots and check the lines, was a real bitch. And then there was wondering about what the NVA might be doing or preparing to do. In time I got used to the routine, but it never got better.

I still have my Snoopy.

- 7 -

Camp Carroll

Next morning, we choppered out. I went out on the last bird with about half a squad. Evacuating a fire support base, even a temporary one, was something I never got used to. The day before, there were roughly four hundred Marines on Henderson. When the last bird was coming in to take the last of us off, there were eight men, one of whom was me.

The NVA clearly knew we were there. They lived in the jungle and would have been both deaf and blind not to see and hear our artillery firing, helicopters taking off and landing, men burning trash, a California state flag, whatever. There were endless clues. Yet at the end of a lift-out, when there were seven or fourteen or even thirty men left, suited up and thinking about getting on a chopper, I never saw the NVA attack. Were I NVA, I would have had a rocket team standing by for the departure, ready to run hot rounds up the pipes of the last choppers off the hill. It would be a cheap and easy victory, and for the Marines, very demoralizing. I'm glad the NVA tacticians didn't think as I did.

Camp Carroll was a major artillery base about five miles southwest of Henderson. It had been there for quite a while. It had strong-back tents, a heavily sandbagged base operations center, and a lot of heavy guns. The guns fired off and on all night. If Marines were in contact with the enemy somewhere, the supporting fire missions could last half the night. If there was no other action, every half hour or so, a big gun would fire out into the night somewhere for harassment and interdiction, designed to keep the enemy on his toes. I had no idea whether H&I fire accomplished anything. I still don't.

Once we all got to Camp Carroll, the Skipper assigned sections of the perimeter to each platoon. As best I could tell, Carroll was a permanent artillery base, and rifle companies rotated through from time to time to provide security for the big guns.

Little and I surveyed our section of the perimeter, got the men in place in already-prepared bunkers, and headed back to the tent where the company officers and senior NCOs would be sleeping. We passed by a sandbagged block building that looked like the bar at the Seabee base. The door was open. A sign over the door read, "Staff and Officers Club." Little and I turned and walked in.

A man behind the bar asked, "What'll it be, Lieutenant?" I wasn't wearing my gold bars, but as the youngest-looking guy in the crowd, my rank wasn't difficult to guess.

"Bourbon and water," I said. Beer was my favorite drink, and I didn't particularly like hard booze, but this wasn't a small neighborhood bar. It was small, but it was brightly lit and crowded. Bourbon seemed to suit the occasion.

I don't know what I expected, but what happened next blew my mind. The bartender got a big milkshake cup, probably twenty ounces, packed it tightly with crushed ice, and filled it with bourbon. I have no idea how much bourbon, but it was a lot.

He put the cup on the bar.

"One bourbon and water, Lieutenant."

"How much?" It couldn't be cheap.

He raised his eyebrows briefly, then smiled indulgently.

"No charge. Happy hour."

"Sure," I replied, as though I knew it all along.

Little got one just like it, and we headed back to the company area. When we walked into the staff and officers' tent, the Skipper looked us over.

"What are you two drinking?" he asked.

"Happy hour at the Staff and Officers Club, sir," Little volunteered.

The Skipper looked around. Washburn and Roberts from first and second platoons, with their platoon sergeants, had arrived before Little and me.

"Gentlemen, you're with me. Lieutenant Davis, you and Little are in charge here."

They all headed for the club.

I turned in an hour or so later, feeling very mellow. I never heard the others return.

– 8 –

3MARDIV

During my tour, the Third Marine Division, of which my regiment was a part, was assigned an area of operations at the spine of the dragon in Quang Tri Province, the northernmost of the provinces in South Vietnam. Immediately to the north was the demilitarized zone, which we didn't "militarize" while the enemy did, something the international community and the American press didn't seem to notice or care about. The area within about ten miles of the coast was populated, consisting mostly of rice paddies and villages. West of the lowlands was the Annamite Mountain Range, running north to south, and in that area forming the border between South Vietnam and Laos. It was mountainous jungle with no population.

The indigenous tribes, the central highland people the French had called Montagnards, had long since been unhappily forced to resettle in the lowlands. Biologists say that the mountains are covered by a tropical rain forest, and I suppose that's true, although I'm not sure I know the difference. When I think of a tropical rain forest, I think of birds, animals, insects, triple canopy vegetation, vines, dead leaves, rain, and mud. I think of a dark and foreboding place. To me, a jungle is the same but perhaps darker. It was a jungle to those of us who fought in it.

The division had three infantry regiments, the Third, Fourth, and Ninth Marines. It also had artillery, trucks, reconnaissance, and assorted administrative and support units. Its headquarters and "the rear" were divided between Dong Ha and Quang Tri, two small coastal cities about ten miles apart.

The Third and Fourth Marines were assigned areas of operation in Quang Tri Province, mostly in the lowlands. The Ninth Marines, of which my little command was a part, was the division swing regiment. When enemy were spotted by reconnaissance patrols or from the air, a unit from the Ninth Marines—a company or a battalion—would be sent to deal with them. I guess the idea was never to allow the enemy to feel safe in any spot outside their sanctuaries. It was cat and mouse, but it was not a game.

− 9 −

VCB

After a week or two patrolling and fighting in the mountains, dancing face-to-face with the North Vietnamese Army, we would be choppered back to a forward staging area called Vandegrift Combat Base—VCB—and named in honor of General A. A. Vandegrift, who led the First Marine Division to victory over the Japanese at Guadalcanal in 1942. Earlier in the war, VCB had been a small semipermanent spot known as LZ Stud. By 1968 it had grown into a major staging area with some permanent structures, mostly sandbag-clad bunkers, and a lot of tents. It was on Highway 9 at the edge of the lowlands, where the mountains started rising westward. Highway 9 was a dirt road and not a good one. Every highway I saw in Vietnam was dirt. I was told there were paved roads in built-up areas. I never saw one.

Supplies were brought to VCB from the division rear at Quang Tri City. I didn't know what to think the first time I saw a truck convoy entering the wire at VCB. Two or three combat engineers led the way, walking and sweeping the dirt road with metal detectors gingerly testing for mines, followed by a couple of M-60 tanks, then the trucks. A couple of tanks brought up the rear. Invariably a flatbed truck carrying a quad-50 machine-gun system anchored the center of the column. A Marine on a swivel seat manned the guns, and to me, looked very much alone sitting there with no protection but his guns. Granted, four .50 caliber machine guns made for a formidable weapon, but this kid sitting in the open would make a tempting target for snipers. Since the entire convoy moved at the plodding pace set by the walking engineers, I always wondered how many quad-50 gunners, or engineers for that matter, got picked off.

The supply guys kept us in food, water, ammo, and mail. The rest was hit or miss. Sometimes we got new uniforms. The men never wanted new uniforms, especially boots, unless their boots were disintegrating. Fashion ruled over comfort; nobody wanted to look like an FNG. I made my men wear new uniforms when we could get them. Otherwise, the uniforms rotted in the humidity and lack of cleanliness.

We got a break from C-rations at VCB when the trucks brought hot food in insulated vats, but that was not the usual fare. VCB was anything but a place of comfort. There was no pavement—only dirt or mud. The large tents had dirt floors, which usually meant mud. The dust and mud alternated depending on the weather. The heat was unremitting. VCB had a shower, an outdoor contraption with no walls, only pipes on posts that somehow sprayed water down on twenty naked men at a time when it worked, which was not often, with water that was usually not hot. The troops were housed in leaky tents and fed in a mess hall, also a tent, with chow from vat cans trucked out from the rear.

The men got package mail, some of which invariably contained a bottle of forbidden whiskey, which the officers tried to confiscate, or at least tried to take steps to see that some degree of sanity prevailed at the party. Unfortunately, there was one tragic incident at VCB caused by our failure to find a bottle that arrived. A Marine private had been sent to us from First Division. He apparently had been in country for some time. I never found out why, but he suddenly appeared in my platoon. He arrived late one afternoon, and I planned to talk to him first thing the next morning. That didn't happen. The kid had brought a revolver with him. That night when he and some others had the bright idea of playing Russian roulette, he killed himself on the first trigger pull. Nobody admitted being a participant, and nobody would say where the booze had come from, like it just magically appeared. One guy said the dead Marine brought it with him. Perhaps. More than that, I cannot say. I hate to admit it, but I felt then and feel now that if somebody was bound to die through his own stupidity, I would rather it be someone I didn't know. That's sad, but it's real.

At VCB, there was no legal liquor, no cold beer, no women, no nothing but a place to sleep uneasily on a cot until the next liftoff. The base was reasonably secure, but the one thing we never got there was relief from the war. The jungle was always out there, and we always knew that soon we would lift out for more patrolling, more enemy contact, more fighting, more heat, more thirst, more going over the same ground, more injuries, more death, more, more, more, more of the same, again and again and again. It was never far from your mind.

Author at VCB, November 1968

— 10 —

First Blood

We stayed at Camp Carroll for only a few days, after which they choppered us to VCB, where we set in for the night in tents with mud floors.

Next morning the company gunnery sergeant stuck his head in my tent.

"Looks like today's the day, Lieutenant."

"What do you mean, Gunny?"

He fixed me with a bright blue eye and studied me for a moment. "Today you'll find out what it's all about—your baptism under fire. They're in the hills over there," he deadpanned, looking west. "We're going up."

Soon the Skipper called us together and gave us the order:

"To our west about two clicks (kilometers), the hilltops are covered with grass. On the side facing us, lower down, is jungle. A recon team has reported seeing signs of life around a cave on the eastern face of Hill 304, near coordinates 981487. The map shows a trail going through the area." He shrugged.

"No idea whether the trail still exists. We are to find out what's there. We are at about elevation fifty meters, so we're going up. We will be lifted to the top of the hill and patrol southeast. The order will be third platoon, company command section, first platoon, second platoon. They have promised us four birds. The usual frequencies apply."

The platoons always rotated. First platoon was first out of FSB Henderson to Camp Carroll. Second platoon was first from Carroll to VCB. It was my turn.

I checked my map. They had told us at the Basic School to bring a roll of contact paper to protect our maps. I didn't know what contact paper was, but I bought some and brought it with me. Turned out it was an adhesive plastic that could be used to cover paper to waterproof it. Uncoated paper maps in the jungle were worthless, so I coated my maps. I wondered why the Marine Corps didn't supply contact paper. I located Hill 304 and saw where the target was. We would land on the hilltop and work our way down to the cave.

The choppers dropped us on a hilltop at the first line of hills, where the flatlands ended and the mountains began rising. We landed in waist-high grass at about a thousand feet elevation. The change in altitude didn't make it any cooler. I set up a perimeter until the rest of the company was on the ground. The Skipper walked over.

"Mr. Davis. Go see what you can find. The company will follow in your trace."

"Roger that," I responded.

I put my flank guards out and started downhill, headed east by southeast. The area was open, the grass was not too high, and visibility was good. After about a half-hour, we reached the edge of the jungle and started in.

"Kilo three, kilo six, over." The Skipper, Kilo Six, was calling.

Whelan handed me the handset.

"Six, this is three, over."

"Three, we're going to hold up here in the grass and set up a perimeter on the last small rise you passed over. From here we will watch your back. Call if you need help."

"Understood, over."

"Six out."

I suddenly felt very alone.

My lead squad started into the thick jungle. There was no trail; the point man slowly hacked a trail with a machete. *If there are enemy around, they will hear us from a mile away,* I thought. My flank guards were cutting their own trails. The going was slow. We continued down. After about an hour, Sergeant Williams, with the lead squad, radioed:

"Three, this is three alpha, over."

"Three alpha, three."

"Better come look at this."

"On the way."

I moved past the men at the tail end of my first squad, which had the lead that day. Sergeant Williams was lying on the ground. I crawled up beside him.

"Whatcha got?"

"Big black area about a hundred meters to our south, along the face of the hill and facing east. Looks like a cave."

I looked. I wasn't sure. The jungle blocked out the sun. It was so dark, everything looked black. In the small areas where the sun filtered through, I could see some leaves moving from an imperceptible breeze, but not much else.

"Okay," I said, "let's move east down the hill about a

hundred meters, then turn right and get below it. We will approach it from below. No more machetes, all quiet.
"We'll crawl if we have to."

"Roger."

Basic doctrine: Never attack uphill if you can avoid it. But the cave, if it was a cave, would be difficult to pinpoint from above. I hoped I was right. I radioed second squad to pass the word back for silence. I called the Skipper to give him a situation report, in Marine parlance, a sitrep.

A platoon of forty or so Marines never moved silently. The men wore their packs. They carried water and ammo. The machine gunners carried guns and metal cans full of ammo. The heat was exhausting, and heavy breathing was the norm. Occasionally an ammo can would bang against a rifle butt, followed by a hissed "Shit!" We did the best we could, but it was obvious to me that if there were enemy in a cave nearby, they knew we were coming. A four-man recon team with rifles, ammo, and not much else, plus months of training, could be quiet. My guys couldn't. They never did.

After what seemed like hours, we were below the cave, if that's what it was. I put first and second squads on line facing uphill. I left third squad to our right to stay perpendicular to us as we moved up the hill. They would be my reserve.

We crawled carefully uphill. The mosquitos were everywhere, but we had to ignore them. Sweat blinded our eyes. The ground was a damp carpet of leaves, but some were dry enough to crackle.

When we got to within twenty meters or so of what was indeed a cave, I heard men talking. It was not English. The conversation was surprisingly animated. Maybe they hadn't heard us after all. I listened for a long time. It sounded like three or four voices at most. I got on the radio to third squad, where the rocket team was embedded.

"Three bravo," I whispered, "get me some rockets up here, and quietly."

"Roger. On the way."

I moved a short distance to my right, where I could get a clear view of the cave opening. It looked like it was maybe ten feet across and about that high, although I was below it and couldn't see the floor. I could see what looked like a couple of men, obviously not Americans. The talking continued. The NVA were clueless, apparently. I was amazed. Then it occurred to me that this must be a trap. Surely they had heard us. I knew we couldn't go charging up the hill without first finding out what was up there.

In a few moments, Lance Corporal Jones and one of his rocket men crawled up beside me.

"Jones," I whispered, "you two get over here where you have a clear view of the cave entrance."

The two of them adjusted their positions.

"Okay, on my command, two rockets in the cave."

The LAAW's they carried were self-contained, unlike the bazookas of prior wars. There was no loader, no "feed me!" like in the movies. Jones and his man, whose name I had already forgotten, opened their rockets with a soft click.

While I was concentrating on the cave Staff Sergeant Little had the other two squads ready for action. He was a pro. My mind was on the cave and the rockets. Little was thinking ahead. I was glad he was.

"Ready?"

The two rocket men nodded.

"Fire!"

Two rockets popped off beside me, and in an instant, the simultaneous explosion of two warheads deafened me. I heard screams, then silence. I waited to see if there was any enemy activity. I hoped whoever was there was dead.

Suddenly an NVA soldier with a mangled and badly bleeding leg came running haltingly toward us, his AK-47 barking. Then Sergeant Manning was streaking toward him from my right. From twenty feet, Manning put two bullets in him. Then silence. We slowly crept forward. There had been four NVA sitting in the mouth of the cave. Three were dead. The fourth was Manning's target, now equally dead.

"Three, this is six! Sitrep!" *Uh-oh.* I could tell the Skipper was not happy.

"Four NVA in a cave, six. We got them. Sweeping the area for any survivors and anything interesting, over."

"Need help?"

"Negative."

"Six out."

We spent another thirty minutes looking around. The dead men were apparently an isolated team. I didn't know what they were doing there, but from any tree near their cave, they could get a clear view of the base we had left a few hours earlier. They were probably there to adjust artillery or rocket fire. I later learned that VCB had been taking rocket fire recently. A recon team had been sent to look for whoever was calling in the rockets. Third platoon took them out.

Now I was seeing dead enemy for the first time. They had on uniforms, had rifles and small bags of rice. It was grisly. They were badly messed up. One man's chest had been opened like a tuna can. There were extensive injuries to their limbs, and on one man's head, brains were showing. There was blood everywhere. It looked like both rocket warheads had impacted just above them, spraying shrapnel all over. I knew I would eventually see carnage like this, but when it was in my face, it was sobering. I felt like I should have felt some sense of elation, but death is sobering when given the chance to think about it, even in war.

We collected their radio, anything in writing, and anything that looked like it might have intelligence value, then made our way back to the company, mostly by the way we had come. I thought about the dead men, but then I didn't know what to think. Their sense of duty was no less than mine, but they were in the business of killing Marines. It's hard to hate a corpse. *Somehow, I'll have to sort all this out, but not right now.*

We moved into the company perimeter.

"Sergeant Little, have the men spread out and take a break while I report in. Jones, great shooting. You too, Sergeant Manning."

Jones grinned; Manning shrugged.

I found the Skipper sitting on a little knoll.

"Tell me," he said.

I told him what had happened. He sat there was a long time, looking first at me, then gazing east toward the base down the hill. Then back at me.

"Lieutenant Davis, you will not ever initiate an attack, even a rocket attack, without first telling me." He wasn't yelling, but it was obvious he was not pleased.

"Yes, sir," I said, somewhat sheepishly. Hell, for what little I know about how the game is played, I thought I handled it pretty well. Now I get a butt chewing.

He paused again, looking at me, then grinned.

"Anyway, it sounds like you did it right. Next time keep me in the loop. You'll do fine. That's all."

As I was getting to my feet, Little came over. The Skipper looked at him.

"Pretty neatly done, Skipper."

Little's endorsement meant a lot. The whole thing happened so fast, I felt like I was on top of it but at the same time didn't know what the hell was happening. I got the rockets in place while Little was getting the rest of the men ready. Somehow it worked.

The choppers picked us up where they had dropped us earlier and took us back to VCB.

That night I talked to Little. I ranked him, but I was smart enough to know I should seek advice from a man who knew the ropes. And I had to rely on him for now and knew it.

"What do you think?"

"I'm impressed."

"No, seriously." I wasn't fishing for compliments. It had worked out. Mission accomplished and all that, but I still wasn't sure I had done it right.

"I'm not bull shitting you, Lieutenant. That was as neat a little operation as any I've seen."

"Thanks, Little."

I didn't know what else to say. I knew he was preparing the men to attack, if necessary, while I was dealing with the rocket team. I would talk to him more when I got a better feel for our relationship. Right then, I was feeling satisfied but a little confused at the same time. It had all gone by in a blur. Anyway, it looked like I had passed the first test.

I sought out Sergeant Manning.

"Where did you come from?" I asked. "I saw one coming toward us, and a second later, you blew him away."

"I was with third squad coming down the hill on your right," he said. "We knew something was up because you had called for rockets, but we couldn't see anything. Suddenly *Boom!* and here's this gook shooting. I just jumped up and got him. Guess I saw him first."

I looked at him. This was the platoon guide, the guy I thought looked older than his age, maybe a little soft, the guy I thought belonged in payroll, not the infantry.

"You probably saved us from a bad result. Hell, he could have shot any of us, including me. Well done, Marine."

"Thank you, sir."

I was beginning to accept that these men were professionals. They knew what they were doing. I hoped I would live up to their expectations.

Over the next weeks and months, I would learn that there were a lot of ways to do things. Sometimes the schoolbook solution was right; sometimes it was wrong. Schoolbooks didn't teach judgment, or adaptability, or insight, or a thousand other intangibles. Those things came to you, or they didn't. If they did, you might live and keep your men alive. If they didn't, you got fired if you lived. But you might go home in a box either way.

Too often, it was just luck.

Author on FSB Pete, October 1968

— 11 —

Race

The next afternoon I asked Jones about the "Nguvu Za Weusi" written on his flak jacket, which he said meant Black Power in Swahili. He had also written, "I'll Say It Loud, I'm Black and Proud." Dr. King's death, coincidentally on the day before I graduated from Basic School, brought a lot of anger, even into the Marine Corps. Jones's declaration was just part of it.

In 1964 I was a freshman at the University of North Carolina at Chapel Hill. James Farmer, leader of the Congress of Racial Equality (CORE) had chosen Chapel Hill as his base for bringing the civil rights movement into the Carolinas. Chapel Hill was a university town and was generally progressive, but there were some famous restaurants on the outskirts of town that were segregated. I manned the barricades at the restaurants alongside other students and CORE members. *The Daily Tar Heel* published a full-page advertisement containing the signatures of students who opposed segregation. My name was first on that list. I am not saying I was one of James Farmer's lieutenants. Indeed, I was simply a face in the crowd participating in his army.

I had grown up in segregated northern Virginia (at a time when the entire United States was segregated to some degree), but as a kid, I was personally a stranger to racial discrimination. I went to elementary schools on military bases and having Black kids in class was not something I ever gave a thought to. They were just other kids. As I got to middle school, I became aware that civilian Virginia schools were segregated, but as a kid, that really didn't register with me. By the time I got to college, I knew better, so I supported CORE and James Farmer. Many, if not most, of my classmates, did not.

I gave Jones a brief outline of my personal experience in the civil rights movement, such as it was, to assure him that I was not discriminating and that it did not bother me in the least to have Black Marines in my platoon. In fact, at that time, I had two Black squad leaders out of three, and one weapons leader out of two, meaning my primary subordinate leaders were Black. Jones was the rocket section leader, a crucial part of my team. I also told him that I did not object to him having something important to him written on his flak jacket, which was undoubtedly against some rule, but we were fighting a war. I depended on Jones and the others, and that kind of rule was not my concern. Still, the enemy didn't care whether there was black power, or white power, or Marine power. We were in it together.

"The enemy doesn't care what color you are, Jones. They just want to kill you. While I sympathize with the plight of Blacks in the United States, and I truly do, this place in this war is not the place or time to be involved in the civil rights struggle unless you discover some racial discrimination in this platoon. If there is, it won't be from me, and I will want to know about it."

Jones stared at me for a moment and then said, "Sir, I understand what you're saying, but I am black and proud of it."

"That's fine," I said. "Of course, you are. Be proud of who you are. But we're fighting a war to the death, and it isn't about color. I will treat you exactly the same as I treat any Marine, because to me green is the only color that matters."

"Understood, sir."

"Then you will understand that I'm going to tell you to have your hair cut regulation short and that the only reason for my doing so is because it's too long, not because it's an afro. I'm going to tell you, and I am telling you, to get a haircut like every Marine is required to do."

Jones looked at me again, and I could almost see the wheels turning in his head. I guess he must've believed that I had no intention of treating Blacks unfairly because he lightened up considerably.

"But, sir," he said, "this is my trademark."

"Trademark or not, Jones, you're going to cut your hair like all other Marines. When you leave the Corps, nobody will care how long or short your hair is, but here it needs to be regulation length. Get with Doc, and soon."

"Aye, sir."

Doc was responsible for the general health of the platoon, and that included his side job of barbering. He had a set of old hand-operated hair clippers and gave free haircuts to the men about every other week. I would wait for a day or so to see if Jones had done what I ordered.

Later that day, I talked to Staff Sergeant Little about the racial makeup of the platoon.

"Do we have any problems?" I asked.

"No, sir," he replied.

"So, the fact that the majority of squad and team leaders are Black has not caused any problems with the white Marines?"

"No, sir. These are Marines, and they act like Marines. The Black squad leaders are no different from the other squad leaders. They're all professionals and understand what we're doing here.

Jones got his haircut the next day.

       ❊ ❊ ❊

As we have all learned over the years, race became a real problem in the months and years to come, particularly in the rear areas where death did not lurk around every corner, and where troops had time to let things fester. I never saw that in the jungle.

On a date I don't remember, but a few months into my tour, a battalion staff officer, a major, came out to talk logistics with the Skipper. While on our little hilltop, he happened to notice Jones's flak jacket inscriptions and asked who he was. He then hunted me down. He expressed his outrage that such garbage was allowed in my platoon and swore that he would see to it that it was stopped. As a young second lieutenant, I was in no position to argue with a superior officer. The best response I could give him was that I would take care of the "problem" when ordered to do so by someone in my chain of command. The good major was not happy but recognized reality. He ranked me but did not command me. Besides, he spent his tour in the rear where he had plenty of time to worry about things other than surviving. What happened after that I never heard. Jones never changed into a different flak jacket.

– 12 –

Happy Birthday

The Marine Corps celebrates its birthday every November 10. On that date in 1775, the Continental Congress passed an act calling for the formation of a battalion of Marines. The Birthday Ball is the social event of the year. Marines attend in their dress blues, their formally clad companions on their arms. The Marine dress blue uniform is perhaps the most recognized uniform in all the United States services. Officers wear a form-fitting navy blue coat with a choke collar (in an earlier time the collar was made of leather to protect the neck from sword strikes, hence the nickname Leathernecks) and gold buttons with ribbons, badges, and medals. The trousers are a lighter blue with a red stripe—the Blood Stripe—down the outer seam. In parades and other formal occasions, officers carry a sword, the curved Mameluke sword, patterned after the sword awarded to Lieutenant Presley O'Bannon in our brief war against the Barbary pirates along the north coast of Africa in 1815, "The Shores of Tripoli."

Even the youngest Marines wear dress blues. The blue coats of enlisted Marines boast a wide white belt, red piping, and gold buttons. Noncommissioned officers wear the blood stripe on their trousers. The Birthday Ball is likely the young Marines' first formal event since their senior prom, and they cut impressive figures in their blues.

The men in my OCS class were commissioned on November 9, 1967, and we went to our first Birthday Ball the next night. For us brand new lieutenants, it was not as formal as it might have been. We had not been fitted for our dress blues yet, so we went in our Service A greens, the daily office uniform. And we didn't sport ribbons and badges other than the National Defense Service Medal, awarded to all active duty personnel in all services. It represented the nation's thanks for service during the Cold War. We called it the "I was alive in '65 medal." I still have mine.

Only a few of the new lieutenants had their wives with them, and after having been effectively locked up in training at Quantico, Virginia, for ten weeks, nobody else had a date. But formal or informal, we had a good time. The beer and booze flowed, and at least we were finally officers and not lowly officer candidates.

My second such event, which I cannot in good conscience call a Birthday Ball, was significantly less formal. On November 10, 1968, Kilo Company was saddled up, sitting in the rain at VCB waiting for helicopter transport to launch us into Operation Scotland II Afton. Recon had reported NVA in the Da Krong River valley and surrounding hills. Our job was to find them. The weather was so bad that the helicopters couldn't fly, so we sat on the helipad for the better part of the day waiting for the weather to lift. Getting rained on was part of the Vietnam experience. I sometimes wonder how we survived the daily downpours out in the jungle with precious little cover. At least this day's inconvenience broke the boredom of waiting for the choppers that never came and gave everyone something to gripe about.

Around midafternoon, a truck bearing a cake arrived. If we couldn't have a Birthday Ball, we could at least have a ceremony. Cutting the Marine Corps birthday cake is a solemn affair, done in a ballroom in dress blues using the curved stainless steel, beautifully inscribed, Mameluke sword. The senior officer holds the sword high for all to see, then carefully cuts a single piece of cake, immediately presented to the oldest Marine present. The second piece goes to the youngest Marine, followed by the third piece to the guest of honor.

Our cake was unceremoniously delivered to the company commander, who cut it with his K-Bar knife. His knife, like those carried by the rest of us, was filthy beyond imagining, but that was of no concern to anyone. Somehow the first sergeant had the names of the oldest and youngest, so we had a sort of ceremony despite the war.

Tradition is important in the Marines; it is passed down from one generation of Marines to the next. It is part of our training. It is about things like knowing where the officer's sword came from, or the origin of the name Leatherneck, or Devil Dogs (teufelhunden, a name given us by the Germans in the First World War), or the 1848 attack by Marines on Chapultepec Castle in Mexico ("The Halls of Montezuma"). It is all the Marines have ever done despite inferior equipment. It is "First to Fight." It is death before dishonor. It is esprit de corps. It is all of those and more.

Something about Marine Corps tradition binds us all. There is no such thing as an ex-Marine or even a former Marine. "Once a Marine, always a Marine" is trite but nonetheless true. The warrior spirit that began in the fighting tops of our ships in the American Revolution has never dimmed. Being a Marine is all about pride of service. The other services make jokes about us but seem always to deliver them with respect mixed with envy. Marines adapt and improvise. They do more with less. They run toward the enemy. It has been that way for more than two hundred years. Tradition of that kind cannot be ignored. It becomes a part of every Marine. It motivates. It endures.

Cutting a soggy cake in the rain with a K-Bar at VCB on the Corps' birthday in Vietnam seemed perfectly normal. Tradition demanded it.

— 13 —

Up the River

It takes six or eight CH-46 helicopters, in multiple lifts, to move an entire company of roughly two hundred Marines. The CH-46 was supposedly designed to carry a rifle squad of thirteen combat-armed Marines, so theoretically, a rifle company could be put on the ground quickly. We were never so fortunate. In Vietnam's thin, hot mountain air, the pilots were lucky to coax up enough lift to carry eight Marines. The day after our 1968 birthday celebration, when the weather cleared somewhat, and we were ready to go, only two choppers showed up for the launch of Operation Scotland II Afton. Since I had the assault platoon, one chopper took most of my first squad, which like most thirteen-man squads in combat totaled ten men, and the other chopper took me, Big Mike with his radio, Doc, the rest of the first squad, and one of my machine-gun crews. I had two helicopters to carry sixteen men altogether for the assault wave, which is plenty if the LZ is not hot. The well-known image of Huey helicopters descending on the enemy like a swarm of grasshoppers seemed like Hollywood, and if it really existed, it was done by the Army. The Marines, then as now, did more with less.

Our landing zone was an unnamed acre-sized clearing on the east side of the Da Krong River. The two helicopters landed in tandem, facing south, and dropped my squad-size platoon in the clearing. As we ran down the ramps, we came under small-arms and mortar fire. The rifle fire sounded like it came from the hills to the east of the river, but in that steep valley, it was difficult to tell. I moved the men on my chopper toward the jungle on that side of the clearing, where at least we would have some cover. Unfortunately, the men on the other chopper couldn't hear me in the noise and confusion and ran in the opposite direction, to the riverbank.

The situation was not favorable. The choppers were gone. We were alone. My little force was split in half. If NVA were across the river, the men on the riverbank were easy targets from behind. If the enemy was present in force above us to the east, we were probably outnumbered, and we had little cover. I yelled to the guys on the riverbank to join the rest of us, but the noise of gunfire and incoming mortar rounds drowned me out. I had Big Mike with me, and the squad leader on the riverbank had a radio, and they finally made contact. He got his men off the bank and got to my position without taking any casualties. I laid out our unhappily small perimeter on a tiny hill just inside the jungle and told everyone to start digging while I tried without success to reach my company commander. We were out of radio range.

I was in charge, and I had few choices. The enemy knew where we were. I had sixteen men—fourteen rifles, my pistol and Doc's, and a machinegun. I could attack up the hill, but because we were in a deep valley, I could not tell where the enemy fire was coming from or from how far away. The hilltop was roughly a thousand feet above us. The jungle was so thick they could have been fifty feet or a half-mile away. Since they were using mortars, they had to be some distance away, but it was impossible to say how far. The size of the enemy force was unknown, I had no contact with anyone, and I had no idea when or if the choppers would return. It was obvious that our only real choice was to stay put and beat back the enemy if they attacked. I didn't have to tell the men to hold their fire until the enemy showed up. We had only the ammunition we carried with us, and we could not afford to waste it shooting blindly into the jungle.

By the time we were consolidated on our little hill, the rifle fire had stopped, but the mortars kept up the shelling. One of my men took a piece of shrapnel in his shoulder, and Doc treated him while we waited. Waited for what? An attack? Relief with the arrival of more Marines? We didn't know; we just waited.

Within about twenty minutes, even the mortars stopped, and shortly the two choppers returned, carrying sixteen more men. They made two passes across the field while their door gunners sprayed the jungle with machine guns, hitting the trees above us. They passed so close above us the guns were spitting empty brass cartridges on our heads. The bullets ripping through the trees above us sounded like a giant scythe going through a cornfield. Big Mike had his radio frequencies and was finally able to tell the choppers we were below them to the east so they wouldn't shoot at us. I popped a green smoke grenade just to be sure, and we tried to melt into the earth until the firing stopped and the choppers landed.

This flight brought my second squad, part of my third squad, and the company commander. I ran into the clearing to direct him to our position. The enemy started shooting again. A mortar round landed on the far side of the river, and a piece of shrapnel carried far enough to knock me to the ground. It had grazed my mouth, splitting my lip. It broke off most of one front tooth and cracked the other. Luckily, I was at the far edge of the mortar round's kill zone. The military term for the kill zone is the "circular area of probability," one of my favorite euphemisms. I was glad I was outside the circle, so the shrapnel had lost velocity. It could have been a lot worse.

The enemy fire tapered off, and the choppers brought in the rest of the company. My wounded Marine was put on one of the helicopters. We moved to a more defensible hill on the south side of the clearing and dug in for the night. Doc put a butterfly bandage on my lip and gave me a shot of penicillin. I declined the Skipper's offer to be medevaced. My lip wasn't bad, and my teeth could be taken care of some other time.

After I placed my lines that evening and had time to think, the day's events began sorting themselves out. This was the first time I had been wounded, and I counted myself incredibly lucky that I wasn't hit in the eye, or that the mortar round with my name on it hadn't landed closer. The thought of what might have happened, beyond being slightly wounded, was frightening. I downplayed the whole thing to my men, but that was false bravado. They knew that being cut off in enemy territory, out of touch, with a tiny force, known to the enemy, was not a happy situation. I didn't feel the gravity of it until it was all over, but then the feeling hit me hard. I knew we would never have been abandoned, but I also knew that the choppers couldn't fly if the weather turned bad as it threatened to do.

My little sixteen-man force was fifteen miles from the rest of the company with jungle and mountains separating us. My retrospective musing about having to fight off an attacking NVA force of unknown size with a reinforced rifle squad was more than a little disturbing. No doubt we would have given as badly as we got, but if we were seriously outnumbered, the prospect was bleak. But we were Marines, and smaller forces have held their ground in worse circumstances. I was ready to fight but was frankly glad it wasn't necessary right then.

The next day my platoon went on patrol. We were sent to look for NVA where the previous day's fire had come from. I didn't expect to find anything since they had not attacked again, but vigilance was the order of the day. It was a slow patrol. At least now, I had a platoon of riflemen with attached machine guns and rockets. We found no sign of any enemy. My best guess is that there was a small NVA team in the area when we landed, and they hit us with some harassing fire and then melted into the jungle.

That was war in the jungle. It wasn't the first time we had one of these inconclusive little engagements, and it illustrates the differences between us and our enemy. The NVA was a professional army, but they had no helicopters, or if they did, they couldn't use them, given our overwhelming air superiority. We moved in helicopters, which were easy for them to spot, or we moved on foot. But even on foot, we had fifty to two hundred men weighed down with all we could carry. The enemy moved on foot also, but unless they were preparing for a major attack or were defending a position, they used four- and five-man teams operating alone in the jungle. They moved at night. They carried their weapons and ammunition and a few small bags of rice and not much else.

They stayed put for days and weeks at a time, waiting for some Americans to appear so they could hit our point man and withdraw into the jungle.

The North Vietnamese seemed to show little regard for the lives of their men, so these little teams were on their own. The tactical advantage of the small teams was surprise. We didn't know where they were. Our tactical advantage was overwhelming firepower, but that was small comfort to the Marine walking point. He was usually the one who suffered when the surprise was sprung.

Mr. and Mrs. America would not stand for their children to be left out in small groups in the jungle like the NVA were, possibly never to be seen or heard from again, so we went full bore. We killed more of them than they did of us, but at the platoon level, every man lost was a personal defeat. There would be many more little contacts like the one by the river, and many of them would be a lot worse.

— 14 —

Mr. D

About three months into my tour, my Marines started calling me Mr. D, a term of endearment and respect that was mysteriously bestowed. I had come to them as a brand new FNG lieutenant. The old-timers, meaning anyone who had been in the bush for at least a month, were always suspicious of FNGs, especially young officers. FNGs were unknown quantities in a place where familiarity and experience mattered. When the FNG was your lieutenant, you had to worry about him because you had to follow him. They had called me lieutenant for a while, or sir, as military decorum required. Nobody could explain why I became Mr. D, but it happened in the unfathomable way that troops decide things. One day they just accepted me. I guess they decided I made the right decisions when I had to. They knew I was fair in a place where fairness counted, where nobody wanted to feel he had been done wrong if he might be dead the next minute. If you're a good leader, your men follow you because they want to, not because they have to. Somehow, we bonded; they were my men.

I knew a few martinets whose men did not respect them, only feared them. There was one in Kilo for a short time, another lieutenant. On his first day with the company he took his platoon out on a daytime patrol and got lost. He and his men spent the night outside the company perimeter. The jungle was dense, navigation on unmarked dirt trails, or on no trails at all, was difficult, and the maps were not the best, but for an officer to get lost on a routine patrol was inexcusable. We were lucky there were no NVA around because if the lost platoon had been attacked in any strength, the rest of the company would have been called to their rescue. That was not a fun prospect in the dark.

I pitied the guy at first, but I soon realized he was a joke, a bad one. He was a blowhard who fancied himself a leader, but he was just reckless, seeking his version of glory. I will never forget hearing him tell his Marines he was "a man who wanted action." He was a fool, and his men knew it. His "action" would be at the risk of his Marines' lives, and we had plenty of action without trying to find more just to show our manliness. I especially pitied his men, the real subjects of his idea of action. He was with us for about a month before they sent him to some desk job in the rear. He was no leader. He should never have been commissioned. His men didn't call him by his initial. I can only imagine what they called him behind his back.

I ran into him back in the States a year later when I ended up in the same unit that he was in. We were training Marines. He had a life-size picture of himself on his office door, thrusting his bayonet tipped-M-16 forward as he jumped, shirtless and too obviously pudgy, toward the camera. He was still the blowhard I had known. Listening to him brag about his combat experience and glory was disheartening. He had, as he forcefully put it, *"been to Vietnam,"* which he must have loved to hear because he said it incessantly. From what I had seen, his tales of his combat heroism were a bad joke, but I saw no sense in challenging him. By mid-1970 the Marines were pretty much leaving the war zone, and our Marines would not be going to war. I just stayed away from him, and he avoided me entirely. I'm surprised he's not a Congressman.

So, Mr. D and his Third Herd had done what was necessary to fight a war we couldn't win while others bragged about their combat prowess. Sometimes I want to puke.

− 15 −

A Day in the Jungle

It is full, black, dark. Clouds obscure any starlight—perfect conditions for the enemy to launch a ground attack.

My eyes fly open. My watch shows 0430. My aching back protests as I shift positions on the hard ground. The plastic ground cloth rustles gently. Big Mike nudges my shoulder. Dawn will soon be pushing its way into what will be a leaden sky. I sit up. Staff Sergeant Little sleeps in a hooch near mine, but he's already squatting next to me.

"Pass the word, stand to," I whisper.

"Aye, sir."

The men on watch quietly nudge their sleeping watch mates. With as little noise as possible, they all get into their fighting holes, weapons ready, pointed down range. I zip up my boots and put on my flak jacket and helmet. I'm already wearing the same clothes I have been wearing for weeks, so there is no need to do anything else. I listen intently for the slightest sound.

Silence. The stillness of the jungle is almost supernatural. No animals. No insects. No sounds. We wait. In an hour, it is full daylight—no enemy to bother us this morning. We have not been hit by a ground attack since I've been here, but the thought, the real possibility, is always there. The relief when they don't attack is real.

"Pass the word to stand down."

I walk my line, checking to see that everyone is up. The men need to shave, eat, and get ready to saddle up.

Back at my hooch, I sit down, and because I'm still half asleep, I go through the morning routine by rote. I take the liner out of my steel helmet, turn the helmet upside down, put it on the ground, and pour in a little water from a canteen. I wet my face and get out what's left of what was once a bar of soap. I make what will pass for suds and lather my face. I make a good faith effort at shaving with a disposable razor that should have been disposed of months ago. Division order: Every Marine in the division will shave daily.

I light a cigarette, find a heat tab, put it in the empty can with holes in the sides I use for a stove, put water in my coffee cup, light the heat tab and put the coffee cup on the stove. I open a C-rat box and find the powdered coffee. The coffee goes in the cup when the water is hot.

I take the main entrée from the C-rat box. Today for breakfast, it will be pork slices. Compressed, processed pork is cut into 3/8-inch-thick slices, each the circumference of the can they come in. There are three in the can. I use my M-38 "John Wayne" can opener to open the can and put it on the stove after removing the coffee cup. The M-38 is an ingenious little device. A short metal blade serves as a handle, and a small, hinged metal tooth folds out to pierce the can lid. A notch just under the hinge keeps the opener hooked around the rim of the can as the device is walked around to cut the lid out. I wear it on my dog tag chain like everyone else. I still have it.

While the pork heats, I open a can of round crackers, the modern equivalent of hardtack. I open a small can of peanut butter and another of jelly. I smear the peanut butter and jelly on two of the crackers and eat them while deciding if I'm hungry enough to eat pork slices this early in the day. I'm hungry enough, so I spear the pork slices one at a time with my K-Bar. There is a small can of pound cake for dessert.

Breakfast over, I gather the trash and throw it in a nearby pit. Any can that has not been opened has been holed with my K-Bar, so it will spoil and not provide food for anyone who may scavenge after we leave.

I report to the Skipper with the other platoon leaders.

"We will be patrolling again today," he says. "First platoon has the day off. Second and third will be out. Mr. Davis, your checkpoint coordinates are 075315, 070310, 059328, 067338. Be at your IP (initial point) at 0700." The check points are based on latitude and longitude as marked on my map.

I return to my hooch. Little and the squad leaders are waiting for me. I give them the day's patrol route while we all study my map. The day's patrol will be a circle to the right. The men write down the checkpoint coordinates.

I give my five-paragraph order:

"We are on Hill 613, here. In thirty minutes, we will move southeast down this finger to the first checkpoint where the map shows a trail. Then southwest along the trail, taking the left fork, to the blue line, then follow the trail in an arc west and northwest taking the right fork, then north up Hill

512, then northeast to intersect the trail we came up here on yesterday, then south on that trail to our current position. It looks like seven or eight clicks, so it should take a good part of the day. No report of enemy activity in this general area for the last three days. The squad order is three, one, two, so Corporal McFarland, you have point. I will follow behind you. First squad to provide flank guards. Our IP will be at the southeast part of the perimeter. Make sure your men have plenty of water. Check their magazines. I have seen dirt caked in magazines recently. Radios will be with me and with second and third squads. Any questions?"

The men go back to their squads. I study my map again, trying to keep everything in one compartment of my brain. I fight this war with a map in one hand and a compass in the other. I know that the trail on the map is most likely long since abandoned and overgrown, and we will be floundering in the bush most of the day. I also know that when we turn southwest, we will be going downhill toward the blue line, a stream of as-yet-undetermined size. On the map, there is an intermittent blue line, but it will not be intermittent. At this time of year, it will be a fairly big stream, probably twenty feet across. Before we get to that stream, we will be crossing a couple of draws, represented by inverted "V's" in the contour lines on the map. The map shows no streams in these draws, but this time of year there will be streams there, so I need to be sure we take the correct stream when we make our arc west and northwest back toward the company position. If we turn too early, we will be off on a wild goose chase.

There is no GPS. It is anything but easy. The real risk is getting lost. If that happens, and we make contact with the enemy, I won't be able to call in mortar or artillery support without the risk of calling it down on my own head. The vegetation is impenetrable. There are no roads, no signs, no nothing. More than once, I have climbed up in a tree and used my compass to triangulate back on any hilltops I could identify to confirm my position. The pressure of navigating in this morass is nearly overwhelming. One false turn can mean disaster. It is also a good way to get relieved of command and be sent to the rear to sit in a bunker monitoring radio traffic all night. That's not what I trained and volunteered for.

The men line up at the IP. We move out in single file, first squad providing a fire team on each flank. I tell Mike to report to six: "IP out." The jungle is not too close here, and we make good time. Hill 613 is really a mountain, Co Tien Mountain, according to the map, and is just over two thousand feet high. On our left, as we move southeast, the mountain drops off almost vertically, so I can catch glimpses of hills to the northeast across the Da Krong River. I can triangulate back on these when we stop for a break.

For the first hour, everything is quiet. I keep checking our position. After about an hour of moving slowly downhill, we start going up. That tells me we have reached a saddle at the end of the finger and should soon be finding the trail on the map. I call a halt and examine my map closely. We have just passed a small draw that drops off to the right. I decide we have reached the trail, which is no longer there. I tell McFarland to take a hard right and start down the south face of the mountain when we saddle up again. I call the Skipper and report the first checkpoint. I am sweating profusely. My mouth is dry. I drink an entire canteen of warm but unbelievably refreshing water.

The break is over, and we head southwest down the side of

the mountain. The jungle closes in. We are paralleling a small stream on my right, which grows larger as it goes downhill. After thirty minutes, I am relieved to make out a relatively open brushy area off to my left, confirmed by lighter green on the map. That tells me we are on the right track. In another thirty minutes, we reach a stream nearly perpendicular to our route. It's a good ten feet across and falling steeply down. The small stream we have been paralleling on my right joins the larger one just above where we are about to cross. This is not the blue line we're looking for. As I predicted, neither of these streams shows as a blue line on the map.

We cross the stream, our boots now wet. We move up a slight rise on the other side of the stream and then start downhill again. The fork in the trail that shows on the map never appears, since there is no trail.

In another hour, the grade becomes less steep, and the ground levels out a little. We are still in the jungle, and visibility is near zero. We have dropped down about 250 meters, or roughly eight hundred feet, from Hill 613. We come to a large stream flowing northwest to southeast. I'm sure this is the nameless intermittent blue line we have been looking for. A smaller stream comes down from my right rear and joins the larger one just in front of me. I call another break and check with Little to see if he concurs with my navigating. We agree we are at the second checkpoint, and I report to the Skipper.

While everybody else takes it easy, I study the map again while smoking another cigarette. I'm certain we are where we should be.

We saddle up, cross the stream, and turn northwest, moving to the end of a small ridge that parallels the stream, which is now on my right. We are following in the trace of what the map shows is a trail, but it is completely overgrown. In an hour, we drop down the northwest end of the small ridge and turn north. The terrain levels out into a valley as the stream we have been following now comes from my right front. Another stream joins in the valley, coming down from the northwest. The map shows a trail splitting off to the left. There is no trail.

We leave the jungle into the open. I can see Hill 613 on my right. This side of the hill is relatively open, and I can almost make out the company position far above me. After another thirty minutes, I tell my squad leaders to set up a temporary perimeter, have their men take thirty, and eat whatever they brought with them, all the while keeping an eye out.

I eat a half-melted candy bar and some crackers left over from breakfast. I am soaked with sweat and very thirsty. I need to drink before I get too dried out. I gulp down half a canteen. Everybody is tired. We aren't carrying our packs, just flak jackets, helmets, ammo, and weapons, but this is hard work. The machine gunners have the heaviest loads, and I want them to rest. I polish off my second canteen. We should be back at the company position well before dusk.

The map shows Hill 512 to my north, and I can see it rising in front of me. There is a gently sloping finger coming down from the hill, which will give us a relatively easy route up. The vegetation looks relatively open. We will follow that finger to the top of 512, which is checkpoint three. I tell McFarland to have his point man be extra vigilant. A rise about two-thirds of the way up the hill at the edge of the jungle will be a perfect defensive position for the enemy. I didn't need to tell him that. We saddle up and move out.

Starting up the finger, we are suddenly in elephant grass.

That is surely not its scientific name, but that's what we call it. I guess it's some species of bamboo. The platoon is making a trail through the grass. It is tall, above our heads. The trail we force through the grass is no wider than a man, and the grass is oppressively near. Tiny saw blades on the leaves tear our arms and clothes. The sun is now shining directly down on us. The humidity is off the chart. There is not a breath of wind. I feel like I'm in a pressure cooker. Sweat pours off me; I empty a third canteen. An hour passes. The elephant grass turns to a shorter type of grass, about shoulder height, increasing visibility. The gradient steepens.

"I'm hit!" rings out after sudden gunfire in my front.

Everybody drops, and I crawl forward. McFarland reports that his point man is down. He has seen three NVA in rough bunkers, but no sign of a large force. Doc rushes past me while two men pull the wounded point man back. We are effectively in the open, but the grass provides some cover as the men spread out. The enemy are still firing, and my guys are laying down a good base of controlled fire. My machine gunners let loose.

Sergeant Manning appears. "Doc says the wound is manageable. Hit in the arm."

I nod. I hear the bloop of an M-79 grenade launcher, followed by an explosion ahead of us. The bloop gunner keeps up his fire. I count six rounds in thirty seconds. That will help keep their heads down.

I don't want to charge up the hill into an enemy unit of unknown size, but I can't stay here in the open. There is no time to call in a fire mission from mortars or artillery because we are too exposed. I must make a decision, and I must make it fast. There is no way to get around on their flank without prolonging our exposure. I won't retreat because we will still be exposed. I really have no choice.

"Third squad on line to my left! First on line to my right! Second squad follow in our trace. Move it! Move it!"

The squad leaders quickly get their men into position.

"I'm hit!" rings out from behind me.

"Corpsman!" several guys yell at once.

"Doc!" I yell, "Get to whoever is hit! Second squad bring him up behind us if you can!"

"On line! Let's go, Marines! Follow me! Keep moving! No stopping! Move! Move!"

Now the Skipper is on the horn wanting a sitrep.

"Mike, tell them we're in attack mode against a small unit, and I can handle it." I pray I'm right.

My pulse pounds in my head. My heart was in my throat at first, but suddenly my body stops giving feedback. I feel nothing. I am concentrating only on running forward. We are all on line, running. Now we're up the hill. McFarland was right. There are three bunkers about fifty meters to our front, just inside the jungle. Bullets are flying everywhere. I hear one flash past my ear, sounding like a sonic boom far away, but lingering. I don't have time to think about it.

Our rush is so fast we catch the enemy by surprise. I guess they didn't think we would suddenly erupt from the grass into their faces. We run, faster, all the men firing. A frag grenade loops neatly into one of the bunkers. Scratch one. By then, the men in the other two bunkers are shot dead.

Everything stops.

"Spread out!" I yell. "Check for more bad guys! Watch your backs! Sergeant Little, make a perimeter while I call the Skipper!"

First, I look for Doc while trying to catch my breath.
"What do we have?"

"Two wounded, one seriously," Doc replies. "The easy one
has a through and through wound with a severed artery in his
left arm. No broken bone that I can find. I got the bleeding in
his arm stopped. He'll be okay. The bad one is gut shot. I can't
tell how bad. I have a compress on it, and I'm starting an IV.
Neither's gonna die unless they go into shock, but they're in
no shape to stay with us."

I call the Skipper.

"Six, this is three. I had a point contact with a small force,
three NVA in bunkers. I have two whiskies, one belly shot,
one with an artery opened in his arm, but he's reasonably
okay. I need medevac for both. We have three NVA kangaroos
(kills). No other bad guys around. I'm about one click from
you, just south of checkpoint three, over."

"Roger three. A resupply just lifted off from here. I'll send
them your way, over."

"Roger, tell them there's a grass landing area, yellow
smoke ... wait one."

"Corporal Gregg," I yell, "helo in the area will pick up
wounded. Estimate ten minutes. Stand by to pop yellow
smoke! Your squad to stay there to provide perimeter until
the helo lifts!"

"Aye, sir!"

"Six, this is three. Smoke ready, over."

"Roger, three, let me know when they're off. Out."

I talk to Doc again.

"They'll be picked up by a resupply, so there's no doc
aboard. Do you need to stay with them?"

"I should go with them, sir. This one needs attention." He

has one of the men holding the IV while he shoots morphine into the man's arm.

"Mike, the handset. Six, this is three, over."

"Go ahead, three."

"Request permission to abort. My doc has to go with the chopper."

"Permission granted. Return by your most direct route."

The company position is about a kilometer from here, almost due east along a saddle connecting 512 to 613. I call Little over.

"Make sure the area is searched. Let the men take a break but keep the perimeter up. When the medevac is gone, we'll move out. Doc's going with the chopper, so we're aborting. Looks like we can go down the finger east of 512 to a saddle, then up to 613. Double-check your map."

"Aye, sir. I already looked at it. Looks like that's an easy trip."

I sit down. It has been maybe fifteen minutes since the first shot was fired. My adrenalin is in super overdrive. My pulse is racing. I'm still trying to catch my breath. I try to light a cigarette, but my hands are shaking too badly. Big Mike reaches over and holds my lighter.

"Thanks, Mike."

"No problem, sir."

The chopper lands below us. Gregg's men get the wounded on board and come up to join us.

I tell Mike to report to six that the helo is away.

Little comes over.

"Good call, Mr. D."

"Maybe," I say. "We were lucky. Nobody killed."

I don't say it, but I wonder what I could have done to prevent a point contact like this. I will worry about that later.

My mouth is parched. I'm still breathing hard, but my heart has slowed some. I am sweating more than ever. I gulp down an entire canteen. That makes four. I have only one left. My other one is back at the company position. I tell Little to get the men saddled up. We need to get moving before more bad guys show up. We move to the top of 512 and look around. I report checkpoint three. We find nothing of interest.

We turn east and follow the saddle back to the company position. It takes about an hour. When we are a hundred meters out, I tell Mike to report "IP in."

We enter the perimeter and move back into our section of the line. I report to the Skipper.

"Tell me," he says. He always says that.

I describe in detail our move through the elephant grass and the point contact. I describe our casualties.

The Skipper nods.

"Sounds like you handled it well. I'll keep you informed when I know something about their condition. Get some rest."

I sit down in my hooch. I had two men wounded. I study my map. I try to figure out how I could have approached the checkpoint at 512 and avoided contact. If I had tried to flank their position from either side, they still would have had a good view of us moving through the elephant grass. They would have been waiting for us either way. If we had come from another direction, they would have vacated their bunkers and met us from behind trees, or perhaps from other bunkers. Their use of bunkers is a bad idea anyway, I think. They are trapped where they are. They can't run. Maybe that's the point. Their superiors won't let them run. Combat by suicide but be sure to take some Marines with you.

The day drags on. I eat another C-rat meal. Before dusk,

we stand to. After full dark, we stand down, and I lie down. I am still playing with possible variations of the day's events when I drift off.

※ ※ ※

Nearly every day of my war in the jungle is a variation of today. Some days there is contact with the enemy. Some days there is not. Some contacts turn out well, some not so well. Some navigation problems are easy, some are not. Today's was somewhere in between. The kid with the belly wound will survive and go home. The other will be back with us in maybe a few weeks. I didn't get us lost.

But the pressure never lets up. I still must navigate in the jungle. I still must make decisions quickly, and my decisions can be a matter of life and death. My men depend on me. I can't let them down.

I never sleep well or for long.

※ ※ ※

Our war was one of constant movement. We would be choppered onto a bald spot on a jungle hilltop. Bald spots existed on the tops of hills and mountains because in some prior operation Marines had cleared it for a helicopter landing zone. If a reconnaissance team was there or had been through it recently, they would report a clear area so we could be sure the LZ was unoccupied. If recon had not checked out the LZ, it might be hot, meaning enemy might be present. Once the company was on the ground and the LZ secured, we would head in whatever direction the Skipper had been instructed, and toward the end of the day we would dig in for the night on a defensible hilltop. The three rifle platoons would form a company perimeter. The guys on the perimeter would dig fighting holes, which two men shared. The holes had to be deep enough for two men to be protected, which usually meant about four feet deep, four feet across, and two feet front to rear. Digging in the jungle with an entrenching tool, a midget shovel we carried on our packs, was not easy. Jungle roots went deep, and often the jungle floor was less than a foot deep with rock below.

The men put out M18A1 claymore antipersonnel mines, usually one for each fighting hole. The claymore was about ten inches long by four inches high and stood on legs that raised it about four inches off the ground. It was curved outward on its long axis. Wire leads ran back to the fighting hole. Squeezing the trigger, which the men called the clacker, fired the claymore.

Claymores were particularly nasty. They were loaded with C-4 plastic explosive against heavy steel on the back side and seven hundred steel balls in front. When fired, the balls would cover an area in a sixty-degree arc out about one hundred meters. It had the effect of a giant shotgun blast. If a claymore detonated into a group of attacking enemy, the killing and maiming was extreme. I had heard stories of enemy infiltration at night where they would crawl in and turn the claymore around, then back away far enough to be clear of the blast before making noise like they were attacking. Whoever hit the clacker would kill himself and a lot of his buddies. I'm glad I never saw that happen.

Once everyone was dug in, we made hooches. Nothing was permanent because we rarely stayed in one spot for more than two days. Our hooches provided little real cover and leaked when it rained, which was most of the time. In our area, the monsoon rains lasted from about October through March. During the night, one man in each fighting hole would be on watch for two hours while the other tried to get some sleep. I did not stand lines but was up many times every night, making sure my men were awake and on watch. The company command group and the mortarmen stayed in the center of the perimeter and did not stand watch.

The enemy always knew where we were. Roughly two hundred Marines in a rifle company, inserted by helicopter, made a lot of noise, try as we may to avoid it. If nothing else, the choppers gave us away. The enemy could meet us or avoid us as they chose. If they decided to melt into the jungle and retreat into Laos, they just disappeared. They knew we had overwhelming firepower if they decided to fight, so their most common tactic was to have a team of four or five men spring an ambush. Sometimes we took casualties, sometimes not. Sometimes we found enemy bodies or blood trails.

The bean counters at the Pentagon demanded body counts, I guess to satisfy the public that we were killing more of them than they of us. We reported what we saw. What happened to those numbers after we reported them is anybody's guess. My guess is they got inflated as they went up the hierarchy, but that may be too cynical. We just moved on to the next hilltop and began again.

We would occupy a jungle hilltop for two or three days while the platoons patrolled the surrounding area, then move, usually on foot, to the next hilltop, then repeat. We were on our feet pretty much all day for at least two out of every three days. Sometimes we would be out in the jungle for two weeks, sometimes for two months. Supplies and replacements came by helicopter. Casualties and the men going home went out the same way. And it rained. It was hot. It was always extremely hot.

After spending a few days to a few weeks in the jungle fighting the NVA, we would rotate back to VCB for short periods, usually two or three days, where we could sleep on cots in tents. That was always a brief respite but never a relief.

– 16 –

Doc

You will never meet a combat Marine who will say the Doc with whom he served, a Navy hospital corpsman, is anything other than a Marine. When the shit hits the fan, and every man is hunkered down, Doc always responds to the cry of "Corpsman!" "Doc" is invariably a title of respect.

Our corpsmen were Navy enlisted men who went through rigorous training to serve as medical assistants. Those assigned to the Fleet Marine Force were given additional training in dealing with combat wounds. They saved many lives.

Over the years, they have served with unswerving devotion and heroism. They have given their lives at astonishing rates: 1,170 in World War II, 109 in Korea, and 639 in Vietnam. For extraordinary heroism in those three conflicts, sixteen were awarded the Medal of Honor, of which four were for action in Vietnam. Two of those four were awarded posthumously. Two Navy ships have been named for corpsmen: a destroyer, USS *Caron*, and a frigate, USS *Valdez*.

Corpsmen are called on to do incredible things, and they do a lot more than stanch bleeding wounds and insert IVs. In late January 1969, my platoon was under mortar attack. That was not so unusual, but on that day, I saw something I will never forget. I heard "Corpsman!" coming from somewhere behind me. Doc, who was behind my radioman, immediately jumped up and ran toward the cry. I followed as soon as I determined that we were not under ground attack.

One of my men had taken a large piece of shrapnel in his jaw and upper neck. He was alive but barely breathing, choking on his own blood and tissue. I watched Doc feel for the cartilage bands in the trachea below the man's voice box, locate the soft strip there, cut a slit in the man's throat, and insert a trachea tube, allowing him to breathe. He saved the man's life.

A tracheostomy is major surgery, done under general anesthesia, in a sterile operating room by a trained surgeon, yet in the dirt and grime and blood of a combat emergency, this nineteen-year-old coolly and calmly did what had to be done.

"Doc, what kind of training did you get to do what you did?" I asked later that night.

He shrugged. "They showed us a film. Then we practiced once on a rubber dummy whose neck had been cut so many times it wasn't hard to figure out what to do."

I am still amazed.

— 17 —

The Load

We carried a hundred pounds and more, including a helmet, flak jacket, personal gear, a rifle or pistol, ammo, food, extra socks, and usually either a heavy brick-sized spare battery for the radios or a 60 mm mortar round, or both. FNGs came out from the rear with extra clothes and even a spare pair of boots. That weight was soon discarded or given to some Marine whose clothes were falling off. Doc carried his magic medical kit. Big Mike carried a radio. The gunners carried machine guns and boxes of ammunition. The rocket men carried rifles and antitank rockets. We never saw a tank. Rockets were not as dramatic as the flamethrowers Marines used against the Japanese in World War II, but I had already seen that putting a rocket in a cave was bad for the health of any enemy there.

We carried our own water. Every Marine carried a coffee cup made from a C-ration can or thermite grenade container, usually with a handle made with wire and an empty .50

caliber cartridge. They were never washed, just filled over and over with reasonably hot water and powdered coffee. We carried little stoves made from a can with holes punched in the sides. Heat tabs provided fuel. Hot coffee in the jungle was a coolant because every swallow caused a gush of sweat. It was inefficient and didn't last long, but there was no other way to get cool. We didn't wear underwear because the heat and humidity caused jock rash from day one. Abandoned skivvies littered the mountains.

We carried our letter writing gear in a plastic bag. It was our most precious possession. Letter writing was constant; postage was free. I wrote to my mother and my girlfriend. My Marines did the same. I made light of everything, saying it was hot, but there was not much fighting. It was all lies, but I couldn't see that it would do any good to describe how bad it was. I even downplayed my first wound, trying to make it seem less than it was. I did not tell them about being alone with a reinforced rifle squad along the Da Krong River. I wonder what happened to that incredible mass of correspondence from the front. I suppose most was thrown away and forever lost.

With all this, we walked up and down hills for hours at a time. It didn't take many weeks for the bottoms of our feet to become hard as shoe leather. We were young and strong, but I don't know how we did it. In thirty minutes or less a man could exhaust himself cutting a trail with a machete. The saw-tooth edges of six-foot-high elephant grass cut like a knife. Come-back vines, meaning anything that grabbed or entangled you, refused to let go. Boots were constantly wet and rotting, which the men hated, because that meant new black boots and looking like an FNG. Uniforms tore because the rip-stop didn't work.

We were issued rain hats to wear at VCB or in the rear and jazzed them up like cowboy or Australian digger hats until the word came down from battalion that the hats had to be worn with the brims down so they would function as rain hats. The hats suddenly looked ridiculous. Even Joe Shit Ragman, the Marines' imaginary version of Sad Sack, looked more squared away. The hats mysteriously disappeared. I mailed mine home. I wear it, brim curled up, when I mow the yard.

We carried it all on our backs, and after walking up and down muddy mountain trails for a few hours, it was ungodly heavy. We would not part with any of it.

— 18 —

Snakes

"Third platoon will patrol to the north. I'll give you your checkpoints in a minute. You will be patrolling along the river. Recon reports no enemy activity, but there is a well-developed trail, so be careful. Report crossing your checkpoints." Skipper's order rarely changed, only the coordinates. In late December 1968, not long after being temporarily left alone in the Da Krong River valley, my platoon was on patrol along the same river, farther south. So far, the patrol had been uneventful. It was hot, as always, and because we were on a fairly good trail, we were making good time. I called a halt for a breather.

Within thirty seconds, somebody in the front of the column emptied a full, twenty-round M-16 magazine. I scrambled to my feet, expecting the worst, but was met with a short silence, then uproarious laughter. I ran forward and found the guys in the lead fire team lying on their backs laughing so hard they couldn't speak. One of them was also on his back, but he wasn't laughing. He was gasping for air and was white as a fish belly. I thought he had been hit.

"What happened?" I demanded.

It took a while to get a coherent answer until his fire team leader calmed down enough to catch his breath.

"This goofball sat down with his back to that tree," he said motioning. "I saw a snake hidden in the bark right next to his face. I kicked his foot and motioned toward the snake. Next thing I saw, he was coming off the ground like he had been yanked up by a rope or something. I swear, Lieutenant, his foot never touched the ground before he emptied a magazine into the snake. Hell, he never stood; he just rose up and turned in midair. Damndest thing I ever saw."

I don't know what kind of snake it was, or whether it was venomous, but it was shredded.

"Good shooting, Marine," I said, grinning.

All this happened within a few kilometers of the company position, and within seconds Mike handed me the radio handset.

"Three, this is six. I heard shooting! Sitrep!"

"Six, this is three. Nothing much. Somebody shot a snake, over."

"Any casualties?"

"Just the snake."

"Six out." I thought I heard a chuckle as he keyed out.

From then this lad was called Snake Shooter. Nobody teased him about it though. His feat became somewhat of a legend in third platoon because the men respected each other, and all wondered if they could have dispatched the snake as neatly and quickly as he had. They also appreciated his giving them the rare opportunity to laugh.

They told us there were over one hundred species of venomous snakes in Vietnam. I didn't believe it. It wouldn't have mattered if there were ten. One was too many.

– 19 –

Not a Healthy Place

Exhaustion was a given. We slept on the ground when we slept, but we were at 50 percent watch when in the jungle, which was most of the time. The platoons took turns patrolling. Two went out every day, so every third day my platoon would stay at the company position where we could get a little rest, although that is a relative term since we were in the jungle and didn't know where the enemy was. We stood watch during daylight as we did at night. When we were in attack mode, there was no rest.

We were never healthy. Malaria could kill, and sometimes it did, but it was not the only problem. Everybody got dysentery, and it never went away. There were no "heads" in the jungle, and when a company of roughly two hundred men stayed on a hilltop for two or three days, sanitation suffered. When you didn't know where the enemy was, you didn't just walk outside your lines to relieve yourself. You dug a hole with your e-tool, then filled it in. Flies were everywhere, and they always seemed to find ways to get to what you tried to hide from them. Biting flies did not appear to mind insect repellant, and they left painful welts.

Any little cut got infected with jungle rot, which is not a scientific term, but whatever it was, it would not heal easily. It was not obviously dangerous, but after a while we got tired of squeezing pus out of the many little nicks on our arms and hands. Doc was hesitant to part with his small supply of penicillin, but when it got bad enough, he would give a shot, and the problem would go away until there were more nicks and cuts. It was not a free pass to the rear, though. It was just part of the daily grind.

Rats were everywhere, big ones, eight inches not counting the tail. A rat bite was a free pass to the rear because it required a series of prophylactic rabies shots in the belly. The guys who went through the process said the shots robbed them of any pleasure they might have drawn from being out of the jungle.

C-rations were nourishing, but their depressing sameness was barely tolerable. Each meal came in a small cardboard box. There was a can with a main course like chicken loaf, turkey loaf, ham and eggs, pork slices, ham and limas, and beef slices with potatoes. The men had some imaginative but not complimentary names for them, like ham and mothers and pig shit pork pies. Each meal had four crackers, some jam, a small can of fruit or pound cake, and a few other moderately appetizing side dishes. And four cigarettes. The food was loaded with protein and was technically healthful, but it came in cans and tasted ten years old, which it may have been. Everyone seemed to go through phases of liking one type of meal to the exclusion of all others, so a man might eat pork slices three times a day for a month until he suddenly decided that one more pork slice would kill him. To me the food was so uniformly tasteless I would seize on a meal that tasted the least bad until one more meal like it would just be too awful to eat. I know I went through the process multiple times. Some men subsisted only on peanut butter and jelly spread on crackers.

C-rations were originally designed for short-term use— something for an army to subsist on until the kitchens could be set up. We didn't have a kitchen. A steady diet of C's led to all kinds of stomach problems, and everyone bitched about it, but we had few choices. Grilled rats were out of the question. Occasionally the resupply choppers would bring vat cans full of hot food, like turkey with all the trimmings on Thanksgiving, but that was the exception. During one operation we were socked in by the weather for more than a week, which meant no resupply, so for several days, we subsisted on captured rice. We came to appreciate the C's a little more but never enough to like them.

Wounds and serious injuries meant a trip to Charlie Med. One thing the movies have right is triage. When a couple of helicopters full of casualties landed at the division hospital, the wounded were placed in one of three groups: one, you can wait; two, you need surgery immediately; or three, you are dead or so close to death there is nothing to be done, because there are barely enough doctors to deal with the second group. It wasn't pretty. The one time I went to Charlie Med, I was in the first group. I didn't mind waiting. I was glad I did not have to make triage assignments.

— 20 —

Native Species

One day in late December we got back from patrol just before nightfall as the feeble sunlight penetrating the clouds was fading to dark. It had rained all day—all month actually. I told Mike to call "IP in." The reply was "Roger, IP in," which meant we were expected and would not get shot at by friendlies as we approached the company position. Once inside our lines, I stood and watched the rest of my men move slowly past me. I knew their fighting holes were half-filled with water and would remain so. They were soaking wet. They were tired. They were exhausted, and like me, stoop-shouldered, expending what little energy they had left just pulling their boots from the sucking mud. We all needed a break from the heat, from the patrolling, and from the rain, but at least we were back inside a friendly position.

Big Mike, who shared a hooch with me, went scrounging in the company mortar section. Sometimes they had extra plastic sheets that mortar rounds came packed in. The plastic could be used to stop leaks in the hooch, and if we could get enough, we could use it as ground cover. Otherwise, we slept in the mud. Big Mike had a way of convincing the mortar guys to part with a few sheets, but there were none left. Our mud floor would have to wait for another resupply of mortar shells.

I made the rounds, making sure my lines were set and that the men were on 50 percent watch, then retreated to my hooch. I was beat. We hadn't seen any sign of the NVA while on patrol that day. All we had seen was rain. The temperature was still in the nineties, but this would be another rainy night—another cold, miserable, rainy night. I wondered how anyone could be so cold in the tropics just by being wet, but I was too tired to worry about it.

Sergeant Manning went to the company area to see if any mail had come in. He came back with a bag full. Mail delivery to the troops was surprisingly regular. The resupply choppers brought us food, water, ammo, and mail. The mail was the most eagerly awaited if not the most important. We hoped for good news from home, anything positive or uplifting, or at least some affirmation that somebody cared, and maybe worried for us. The men wrote home constantly, and the more mail they received, the happier they were. We didn't have USO or entertainment in the jungle. The sense of being cut off from The World was overwhelming. Anything from home was welcome.

Sergeant Manning stopped in front of my hooch.

"Mail for you, Mr. D."

He handed me a couple of letters. One envelope was oversized, and I caressed it gently. My girlfriend mailed me one packet of instant oatmeal almost every day. When several came in at one time, I would hoard them. Oatmeal was infinitely better than C-rats. By the time I had been in the jungle for a couple of months, anything was better. I would eat this one next morning.

"I passed out all the mail," said Sergeant Manning.

"Any bad news?"

"None that I've heard of, sir."

"Thanks, Manning."

Bad news meant a Dear John letter. They came from time to time and gave the men an opportunity to bond. The recipient was allowed—expected—to get weepy for a while. Then he would beg to get sent to the rear to see the chaplain, which was invariably allowed if the tactical situation permitted. After a visit to the chaplain, he would find some way to get roaring drunk. The first sergeant would then load him on the next chopper out, and he would be delivered to us monstrously hungover.

When he recovered, the men would gather. The testosterone-fueled assembly would engage in a deep discussion of love and lost love, abandonment, and despair. After patiently hearing the bereaved man's woes, they would conclude informally that the former dearly beloved was just a common whore anyway, and the bereaved was well rid of her. The bereaved usually accepted their judgment as something he had suspected all along.

I removed my boots and winced as I pulled my socks off, and the loosened skin around my ankles peeled away. I would have to ask Doc for some gauze or something. I squeezed muddy water from the socks. I had lived in France when I was in high school and recalled that French army soldiers called coffee *le jus de chaussettes*—sock juice. I was glad I wasn't drinking this stuff. I shivered; the cold was getting to me. Dry socks would be nice, but there were none. I insisted that the men keep a dry pair of socks in a plastic bag in their pack as I did, but if the wet pair never dried, the dry ones were dry only once. During the monsoon, there was no dry anything. And what was the point of putting dry socks in wet boots anyway? The wet weather was just one more enemy.

I was not surprised to find a leech attached to the back of my left calf. You couldn't feel leeches when they attached themselves to you, but they were in the jungle waiting, so you always looked for them when you could. I took out my lighter and lit a cigarette, while once again promising myself that I would quit smoking if the enemy didn't kill me. I touched the thing with the cigarette. It released its hundred-tooth death grip and fell into the mud. Its anticoagulants had done their job, and blood ran down my leg. The leech had grown from its usual hungry state when it latched onto me—a flatworm about a half-inch long—to the size of a roll of dimes, or anyway a small sausage. I wondered if I would ever want to eat link sausage again, but that assumed I would survive, and thinking about going back to The World invariably brought bad luck, so I dashed that thought.

The leech lay in the mud, not moving. I nudged it with my toe. It was so engorged it couldn't move. Or perhaps the cigarette burn had killed it. *Maybe cigarettes have a positive attribute after all*, I thought. Insect repellant was also good for dealing with leeches. Some chemical in the repellant penetrated a leech's skin and killed instantly. It was most satisfying. The swarms of mosquitoes in the hooch reminded me that I was out of repellant.

I stubbed out the cigarette. No telling what unknown

poison it had somehow picked up from the leech. *No, not on the burning end*, I thought, but by then the cigarette was out.

I unsheathed my K-Bar fighting knife and slid it under the leech. I draped the slimy thing over a smoke grenade, a cylinder about the size of a twelve-ounce beer can. We used smoke for marking positions: green for friendlies, red for enemy, yellow for everything else. I don't remember what color this one was. The leech was so fat it wouldn't bend in the middle. I watched it roll off the grenade.

"Had your fill, asshole?" I muttered, like talking to a leech was normal. There was no response, but then there was no normal, either. I wondered if my blood was clotting inside the leech or if these creatures kept it liquid while they digested it. I couldn't think of why I cared. Then I wondered whether they excreted the unused part, and how, or whether any was left unused, then again wondered why I cared. The absurdity, the absurdity of everything—the leech, the rain, the enemy, the dead and dying, the war—was getting to me.

The leech didn't move. I cut it in two with my K-Bar, which wasn't sharp enough to make a clean cut. Its pressure was enough to tear the leech in half and squirt blood, my blood, onto my hand. I recoiled, like the leech had some way of harming me after being hacked asunder.

I smacked a mosquito. More blood. I grunted at the irony. I wanted to think that on some days Mother Nature spilled more blood in this hellhole than the enemy did, but I was sure it wasn't true. Leeches and mosquitoes were small potatoes when American servicemen were being killed at what we later learned was an average rate of forty-five every day in 1968. I'm glad I didn't know that statistic then.

Another creature that captured everyone's imagination

was the rock ape. The old Tarzan movies of our youth introduced us to the cacophony of jungle wildlife, with shrieks and caws and hoots and all manner of strange sounds, but my jungle seemed nearly lifeless. Birds didn't sing, tigers didn't growl, monkeys didn't hoot. There were insects galore, and plenty of snakes and other crawling creatures, but it seemed that any animal with the ability to get away had gone somewhere else. Except, that is, for the rock apes.

Rock apes were everywhere. They lived in the mountains and in the flatlands. They were tailless, stood over five feet, and were black or auburn or gray, so they blended in with the rocks they lived around. They lived in large groups and were powerful and unafraid. They stayed on the ground and generally walked on all fours, but upright at full speed, they could outrun a man. If you came near a troop of them, they would throw rocks. If they found you sleeping, they would steal anything they could get their hands on. There was a report that a soldier was carried off by an unusually large rock ape and was rescued only when a couple of his buddies tackled the beast. Just about every Marine in Vietnam had at some point seen a rock ape or knew a guy who had or had at least heard of them. Regardless, they all believed they were out there. I never saw one.

I heard a couple of vets talking about rock apes recently and decided to do some research. Not surprisingly, there are online chat rooms where old vets still talk about them. Many say they saw them and describe them in some detail. One guy saw his buddy's arm torn off by one. Others suggest that rock apes are a Big Foot species.

And I suppose not surprisingly, primatologists say there are no rock apes in Vietnam. They say the only true apes in Vietnam are gibbons, which live in the forest between North Vietnam and China, hundreds of miles from where any American ever set foot. Gibbons are tawny red in color, live in trees, and grow to less than two feet in height. One report indicates that there are about 110 cao vit gibbons making their way back from the brink of extinction, and even fewer black crested gibbons sadly on their way to extinction.

Vietnam also has lorises, macaques, and monkeys known as langurs. None are more than two feet tall, and most are far smaller. None are aggressive, and as best I can tell, none throw rocks. All have tails but the stump-tailed macaque, but that one doesn't walk upright, and a large male of that species tops out at about twenty-five inches. None of these primates can carry off a child, much less a grown man. There are large rock apes in Gibraltar, but that's on the other side of the world. So, it is a little strange that seemingly the great majority of the men and women who served in Vietnam knew everything there was to know about an ape that didn't exist, but then a lot of people believe in Big Foot, too.

– 21 –

Ray Davis

When Operation Scotland II Afton ended, I was flown back to the division medical facility at Quang Tri City where a dentist repaired my broken tooth with a temporary crown. The division commander pinned a Purple Heart on me in a quick ceremony in his office, then gave me a ride back to VCB in his helicopter. In all honesty, I would have preferred to stay in the rear for a day or two like everyone else did when they got the chance, but that wasn't an option. The Old Man knew I belonged with my troops. A few months later, when he pinned a second Heart on me, he ordered me not to get hit again. I would obey that order half-heartedly because it meant I would not be returning to my men.

Everyone knew I was the commanding general's son, but thankfully nobody said anything about it. My father, Major General Raymond G. Davis, wore a Navy Cross for his heroism at the bloody battle for Peleliu in 1944 and the Medal of Honor for leading the First Marine Regiment's desperate breakout from the Chosin Reservoir in Korea in the bitter winter of 1950, plus two Silver Stars, a Bronze Star, and a Purple Heart, among many others. Despite his rank and accomplishments, he was a quiet and thoughtful troop commander who rarely raised his voice, was never profane, and loved his Marines. He was also a tactical genius.

In the spring of 1968, he was at Marine headquarters in Washington running the manpower section when the commanding general of the Third Division died in a helo crash. Ray Davis was sent to Vietnam on three days' notice. For a short time, he served as assistant corps commander of the Army's XXIV Corps, which had two Army divisions and one Marine division under its nominal control, and then took over the Third Division. While at XXIV Corps, he was impressed by the Army's helicopter mobility and adapted it to good effect when he became CG of the Third Division.

As coincidence would have it, I had orders to the Third Marine Division before my father was suddenly sent there. That apparently caused some concern in high places. In April 1968 I was about to graduate from the Basic School, when Lieutenant General Herman Nickerson, then chief of staff of the Marine Corps and an old war comrade of my father's, called my mom.

"Knox," he said, "you know Ray is in Vietnam now, and Miles is scheduled to go soon. If you want, I can have his tour delayed until Ray comes home so they won't be there at the same time." My barely five-foot-tall, redheaded, former-schoolteacher mother's immortal response was, "You chicken general, don't you dare put that responsibility on my shoulders!" Pretty brassy of my mom—my brother and I reverently referred to her as "The Queen" behind her back—to call a three-star Marine general a chicken. I didn't hear about this until after I came home. I went to Vietnam as originally scheduled.

When he arrived at the division, Ray Davis knew there was a problem, and he was prepared to deal with it. As the war had expanded since 1965, the NVA sanctuary in the DMZ had become more and more a threat. Americans were not allowed to go there, but the enemy came and went as he pleased. If we had crossed the line, the North Vietnamese, the Russians, and the Chinese would have whooped it up in the United Nations, and the American press would have damned us as the aggressors while conveniently ignoring the presence of the NVA. But they were there, and we were not, and in an effort to seal the DMZ as a route into South Vietnam, the Pentagon created what became known as the McNamara Line, named after the secretary of defense. The Marines built a series of fixed strong points parallel to the DMZ connected by all manner of electronic devices for detecting and combating infiltrating enemy. The McNamara Line had the desired effect of keeping the enemy from coming south, but there are always unintended consequences, and those consequences caused American blood to flow.

The NVA were not stupid. Now that they had fixed targets, they simply moved their well-camouflaged heavy artillery into the DMZ and began shooting at the now-immobile Marines. Whole battalions of Marines occupied—were cooped up in—fixed positions and over time took dreadful casualties. Names of positions like Con Thien and C-2 became nearly synonymous with Khe Sanh, where the enemy pinned down an entire regiment left holding an air strip for no good purpose. Somehow the whiz kids in McNamara's Pentagon refused to understand that a guerrilla war had to be a war of movement and that Marines in particular were ill-suited for sitting still.

Ray Davis had been a battalion commander in World War II and again in Korea, and he understood the tremendous power of a mobile battalion of Marines. His first staff briefing after taking command has become the stuff of Marine Corps legend. He ordered that before dark that day there would be no unit larger than a company inside a fixed position. He understood that his Marines would best be used in the attack, not sitting in a defensive position getting hammered. Jaws dropped. "Who does he think he is?" someone whispered. Didn't he know there were NVA out there?

He knew. The fixed positions emptied, and the Marines went hunting. Over the summer of 1968, many battles produced casualties, but by the end of the summer, there were no large enemy units in the Third Division area of operations. The NVA never attacked through the DMZ while Marines were in the area, and the Third Division was now free to strike westward toward the NVA sanctuary near Laos.

My father arrived in Vietnam in the spring of 1968, after I had already received orders to the Third Division, so I ended up under his command. If being the CG's son had any advantages, I can't think of any. I never felt pressured to be the hero my father was, but I always felt that I was expected to be something more than an effective platoon leader. My men, on the other hand, were not impressed, which was what mattered. They wanted effective leadership, not a hero. They couldn't believe that the CG would send his son into the jungle when he could have given me a cushy job in the rear, but I wasn't there for a cushy job. I had trained to be an infantry officer, and that's what I was.

Earlier, when I was at OCS, I kept mum about who my father was. One day the platoon sergeant was handing out mail and came to a letter addressed to me, on which my father had stamped his return address, complete with rank.

"Davis," he said as he handed me the letter, "somebody told me your old man is a general or some sort of shit like that."

"Yes, Platoon Sergeant!"

That was it. It turned out that everybody knew, but nobody said anything. That was a blessing.

I have always been awed by the moral courage of a man who could send his own son into combat and immediately into harm's way when he could easily have sent me to the First Division and let me risk it under another general's command. But we were both Marines and understood that no favors would be asked or given. I suppose the fact that he later sent me out into the jungle to get wounded twice is proof enough that I wasn't done any favors. Still, I can't imagine how he would have told my mother if I had bought the farm.

Ray Davis loved his men, but he particularly loved the men doing the dirty work. He made sure the supply line went to the bush and didn't stop in the rear. Hot chow went out as often as the weather allowed, which wasn't often. "Gedunk boxes"—packages of candy and cigarettes—went to the Marines in the bush, and God help the supply officer who let one stay in the rear. In late 1968 new camouflage jungle uniforms were issued. The general quietly informed his staff that until every Marine in the jungle had a new uniform, he had better not see one in the rear, and if one appeared there prematurely the man caught wearing it and every senior NCO and officer up his chain of command would answer for it. We jungle warriors got our new uniforms.

The only downside to getting new uniforms was that we all suddenly looked like FNGs, which made having buckskin boots more important than ever. When looking salty is more important than being well camouflaged, logic is yet another casualty of war.

— 22 —

The Heat

If sweat could be bottled and sold, every man and woman in Vietnam would have made a fortune. The country was ungodly hot and humid. In the rain of the monsoon season, it was hot. In the drier summer, it was hotter. I don't remember a day when my clothing was dry, rain or shine. Sweat ran down our faces, our arms, our legs, our backs, everywhere.

The ever-present body odor was worse than walking into the filthiest imaginable men's locker room. It reminded me of living in France in the early 1960s. The French seemed to bathe once a week, whether they needed it or not. The difference was the perfume. We didn't wear designer fragrances; we wore DEET, which was both a blessing and a curse. It was reasonably effective at keeping the ubiquitous swarms of mosquitos at bay. But the enemy could smell it; they had no such luxury. They always knew where we were.

The sweat had to be replaced, which required a lot of water. What I had surmised while in the supply shack was correct. Whenever a chopper carried off a Marine, alive or dead, we took his canteens and passed them out where needed. I soon carried six, as did most of my men, but there never seemed to be enough. We filled our canteens with water from five-gallon cans that came out when the resupply choppers brought food and ammo, but the choppers couldn't always fly.

When the weather socked us in, we filled our canteens with water from mountain streams. The streams were beautiful and pristine, gurgling happily down the mountainsides. They were also loaded with unknown thousands of parasites and micro-organisms and were laced with Agent Orange from the constant spraying of defoliant. A lot of men went home with parasites in their bodies. We all got dysentery, but in that climate, you drank, or you died. You would worry about the long-term effects if you survived. I still worry about the Agent Orange. Today I am mildly diabetic secondary to Agent Orange, or so the VA says. A lot of guys are much worse off. A lot of guys are dead.

The company was trudging single file through eight-foot-high elephant grass one day when I heard "Corpsman!" from somewhere in front. I looked around at Big Mike.

"Did you hear gunfire?"

"No, Sir. Somebody's probably got heat stroke. I've seen it before."

The column stopped. I worked my way toward the front, stepping over exhausted men grateful for the break. I found a Marine from first platoon lying on the ground, face-up, sweating profusely, pale, and clammy. He kicked and heaved while two corpsmen tried to administer CPR. Other men poured water on his face and body. Another ripped at his clothes. He was alive, but within a few moments, he became barely responsive, choking out a few rasping gasps. Despite the frantic action of those over and around him, his gasps became less and less frequent. They got an IV in his arm, and one of the docs injected him with something.

But it wasn't enough. His movement slowed. His face turned pink, then quickly went beet red. The mask of death slowly came over him as the others worked heroically to save his life. By the time a chopper arrived, he was gone.

God, what a shame. The kid was a private, an FNG. His platoon leader, Washburn, was standing next to me, shaking his head.

"Who was he? I asked.

"Name was Williams. Just joined us late yesterday. I haven't had a chance to talk to him. I would have chatted with him tonight; I don't even know where he was from. I assigned him to my second squad. That's all I know."

The kid was overweight, with chubby cheeks and a little roll of belly fat, but not by a lot, maybe fifteen pounds. Back in The World he would have looked like a normal nineteen-year-old, but Marine Corps standards required a different normal. I figured he had finished boot camp looking hard as a rock, as they all do, and then went to infantry training, but somehow between there and his arrival with us, he had taken too many trips to the doughnut shop.

What a poor stupid fool, I thought, then mentally corrected myself. He was a Marine, a dead Marine, simply because he had been sent to this hellhole not looking like a poster Marine. I could picture some sergeant somewhere in the rear saying, "You're fat, Williams, but you won't be in about two weeks. Those mountains will work it off you."

Private Williams' next two weeks would involve

embalming and burial, not losing weight. He would be fat forever.

When the chopper left, it was over. Because the kid was new, nobody had gotten to know him, nobody grieved for him, and nobody missed him. For most, he had never really existed, but for me, he never went away. By the time this happened, I had been in country for about four months and had seen plenty of death, but this was the first time I saw a guy with no visible wounds die slowly before my eyes. I still see his face turning red, his body going rigid, then relaxing, then nothing.

It was small wonder men occasionally died from the heat. In shape or not in shape, the load on our bodies was tremendous.

The heat was not just uncomfortable; it was deadly. And it was ungodly hot.

—23—

Come Clean

I had my platoon out on patrol one day, far out in the jungle, and by midafternoon, we had hit all our assigned checkpoints without finding anything. On the way back to the company position, we crossed a mountain stream we had seen on the way out. It rained in the jungle year-round—all day and night during the monsoon, every afternoon during the dry season—and every little draw had water in it. The stream was about twenty feet wide, with a pond in a flat stretch. Despite the ugliness and heat of the jungle, the stream was beautiful—clear, fast running, clean to the eye at least, and, as we soon learned, very, very cold. I radioed the Skipper for permission to stop and take a swim. We rarely got clean, even at VCB, and the opportunity to take a break in a mountain stream was too good to pass up.

I put half the men in a defensive perimeter and let the other half take to the water. These Marines immediately reverted to the kids they were. The water was desperately cold, but the men stripped and jumped in buck naked, the white asses among them looking like uncooked biscuits. They had water fights, threw each other in, floated on their backs, did awkward cannonballs off a small embankment, whooped and hollered, and acted like ten-year-olds. After thirty minutes or so, I called time.

"Okay, guys, time for the other men. Get cleaned up."

We had no soap, so they scrubbed their bodies with sand. They got out reluctantly and put on their filthy, sweat-soaked uniforms. They were Marines again and took over perimeter duty. The second group, me included, was as crazy as the first. It provided relief for all of us.

When we got back to the company position, I reported to the Skipper.

"Lieutenant, do you realize that every damn gook within ten miles of you could hear the racket you and your men were making?" he demanded.

"Yes, sir."

"I hope you had a secure perimeter."

"We did, sir."

Next morning third platoon manned the company hilltop while the rest of the company, including the Skipper, went to the stream. They were as loud as we were.

Taking a bath in a mountain stream may seem like a small thing, but it was a very big thing. The jungle, the NVA, the wait for the next contact, and the ever-present danger—the thought of death behind every tree—all had a dampening effect on everyone, and it multiplied as the days passed. The daily, hourly tension was oppressive, and there was no relief from it. Even when we spent a day or two at VCB, we were just waiting for the next launch back into the jungle. Only a couple of days in the jungle made us filthy beyond imagining, regardless of how we tried to maintain sanitation. If Marines don't learn anything else in boot camp, they learn cleanliness.

The little lark in the stream had a tremendous effect on morale, at least until we saddled up and moved again. After that day, we did it as often as we could. To this day, I can't pass a mountain stream, or any small rivulet, and not think about what undoubtedly was the best bath I ever had.

- 24 -

Up Close and Personal

One morning on some jungle hilltop, we stood down as it got light and saddled up to move to the next hill for more patrolling or fighting, or both. Moving a company of about two hundred Marines in the jungle is not easy. The main column goes single file on any path that might be there. If there was no path, the point man hacked one with a machete until he was exhausted, which didn't take long. Then the guy behind him would take over. It could take a day to move a couple of miles.

We always put out flank guards—a fire team or more walking parallel to and on each side of the main column. The flank guards also moved in single file, and even if the main column was on a trail, the flank guards were hacking their own. It was hard work, and it was dangerous.

That morning third platoon brought up the rear of the company. We were just out of our former position when the flank guards to my right took fire. Not a lot, just a few rounds.

"Lead and middle squad right! Trail squad close up! With me. Move right. Nobody fires until we find our flank guards!"

I had given this or a similar order more than once. The men knew what to do. I always followed my lead squad when in line, so as we did a right face and moved to the sound of gunfire, I had a squad on each side of me. We didn't just rush headlong at the enemy in a suicidal attack. We worked our way by maneuver, dodging behind trees, running zigzag, and struggling through the thick vegetation for maybe five minutes until we found our flank guards firing into the bush. They couldn't tell me what was out there, only that they had taken small-arms rounds, and one had been hit. I told the fire team leader to get the wounded guy back to the company. The rest got on line with us, and we continued forward. Within minutes we were in a fight with what turned out to be eight or ten NVA. They were well camouflaged, but their muzzle flashes gave them away. Fortunately, as was often the case, they were firing on full automatic, and most of the bullets from their rifles were going into the trees. Machine guns are more accurate and deadly, but luckily, they didn't have any. My guys were now throwing grenades and directing accurate fire as we moved toward them. Suddenly we were among them.

A close-in ground fight in the jungle runs like a nightmare out of control. The confusion is magnified by the unremitting noise of rifles, grenades, mortars, sometimes artillery, yelling, screaming, crying, and dying. The noise overloads the brain. It is physically painful. Nothing follows logically when your visibility is limited to what the jungle will allow, which isn't much. You know there are enemy right in front of you that you can't see, but they are shooting, and you shoot in return. It is total chaos; it is the ultimate madness. For me, it also meant the distraction of being in radio contact with the Skipper, trying to tell him what we were seeing. He had to know what was happening in case he needed to bring more force to bear. I told him, amid all the noise and confusion, that it looked like I could handle it.

When the close-in shooting starts, your first impulse is to get down. A platoon leader doesn't have that choice, or at least he can't just get down and hide. He must know what is happening because he is in charge, he is responsible, and he must lead. I tried to assess where the enemy was, where my guys were, and what the hell was happening. I could see that some of the NVA were retreating, but we were still taking fire, probably from enemy in the trees. There was gunfire everywhere. I yelled for the men to shoot up into the trees. An enemy body fell fifteen feet from me. Then, "Gooks behind us!"

I carried a Colt Model 1911A1 .45 caliber pistol, the officer's standard sidearm, but I drew it from my holster only when it needed cleaning because killing the enemy was not my job. My men did that at my direction. When the shooting first started that day, I had pulled out my 1911 and racked a round into the chamber. Maybe I sensed something; maybe someone was looking over my shoulder, maybe I was just lucky. The war came to me personally when I turned and saw an NVA soldier behind me, eyes widened because I was right in front of him. As he raised his AK-47 to kill me, I put a pistol bullet in his chest from arm's length. I felt his blood splatter onto my hand and at first thought he had hit me. But it was only him, and he died as I watched him recoil from the force of the bullet.

As I instinctively pulled the trigger, I caught the look in the man's eyes—the boy's eyes is probably more accurate, he couldn't have been more than sixteen—and what I saw in them was not anger or hatred or some malignant desire to kill me. I saw fear. I don't know if the kid realized he was about to lose the race to oblivion or if he was only plain terrified. I don't know what he was thinking other than he had to kill me before I killed him. I like to think that when his eyes met mine, he saw an angry, highly motivated, steely-eyed, trained killer, but he probably saw the same fear in me that I saw in him. But I was the killer.

The shooting stopped. The enemy had run or died. We counted four dead NVA. We moved back to the trail. All my guys were alive. We had a couple of wounded, but none too seriously. The Skipper called for medevac. I sent a squad back to the hilltop we had just evacuated to get the wounded on the chopper. They would catch up with us later. Other than my very personal split-second involvement, there was nothing different about this little action than many others like it.

I think a lot about the kid I killed. Using my Marines as a weapon was my job, and they killed a lot of enemy. That's how warfare works, and I have never given that much thought other than to regret the terrible loss of lives on both sides. But killing a man face-to-face is different. Today we are fighting a seemingly antiseptic war involving drones flown from halfway around the world, laser-guided missiles and smart bombs that can go through a window from thirty thousand feet, snipers with increasingly accurate weapons capable of killing at more than a mile, and tanks that can hit an enemy position without ever being seen.

The other side used and still uses equally impersonal

but more primitive booby traps. In Vietnam, they were officially called SFDs—surprise firing devices—an apologetic euphemism if ever there were one. Today the booby traps are called IEDs—improvised explosive devices—as if calling them something technically descriptive makes them any less deadly. Same song, second verse.

Regardless, close combat has not been supplanted, but now as then, killing a man with a rifle from fifty feet, or from a thousand yards, is not the same as killing him at arm's reach while looking into his eyes. I don't think it happens very often. Maybe it does.

I sometimes see the boy's face in my nightmares.

—25—

OP 950

There was a peaceful interlude in my war. In January 1969, I spent three weeks with my platoon posted on Observation Post 950, coordinates 844456. The little outpost itself was terrible. It had been there since the time of the French and was a rat- and insect-infested agglomeration of bunkers, sandbags, and wire, thrown helter-skelter on a mountaintop. It was atop a 950-meter-high mountain—about thirty-one hundred feet. It overlooked the old airstrip and flattened bunkers of the Khe Sanh Combat Base. Khe Sanh had been the scene of great battles and great loss a year earlier. Now it was still. The thousands of bomb craters around it gave it a lunar ghostliness.

The platoon leader whose unit I was relieving briefed me on the situation: OP 950 was surrounded by so many unmarked minefields, placed by so many French and American units over so many years, that it was not safe to venture outside the wire. Being surrounded by mines was both good and bad. It was good because, assuming there were mines out there, the enemy would have a difficult time getting to us. It was bad because it seemed to give the men a sense of complacency. They wanted to let themselves relax, but that was not an option, particularly at night. The worst part was the cold. Three thousand feet elevation is not particularly high, and Vietnam is not a cold place, but at night when the clouds descended and the wind blew, our jungle utility uniforms provided little protection from the wet, clammy air. It was a constant struggle to ensure that the men on watch were staying where they were supposed to be. None of us liked the foggy nights.

On OP 950 we looked for enemy movement, but we saw little more than elephant grass and jungle. Either the enemy moved at night or not at all. Our stay on OP 950 also gave us a break from patrolling. That could have been a bad thing with a lot of young guys together without a lot to do, but all the men got along well. They played cards constantly. They had a game they called Rat Shit, so named for reasons I never learned. It was something like Hearts. I never played, but I watched from time to time. If they were gambling, which was against regulations, I never learned of it. They didn't have any money anyway; there was nothing to buy in the jungle.

We did a lot of training in various tactical maneuvers, and I made sure the men kept their weapons, their ammo magazines, and themselves clean. We got water by helicopter resupply, but bathing was not high on the priority list. It got pretty close after a while. One division-wide rule was that all Marines shaved every day. Shaving with cold water out of your helmet was never pleasant, and the rule seemed somewhat ridiculous on the surface, but looking scruffy, like nearly every Marine and soldier in the movies does, is not a morale booster. The guys bitched about it, but they obeyed orders and looked clean even if they smelled like camels. I include myself in that description.

I was accomplished with a map and compass and was constantly working with my squad leaders to make them more proficient. Getting lost in the jungle was easy. Getting into a fight in the jungle and not knowing where you were was a potential disaster. You couldn't call in an artillery mission if you didn't know where you were, because if your coordinates were wrong, you would become the unintended target.

I spent a lot of time listening to stories of home, parents, girlfriends, wives, children, cars, jobs, and favorite pets. When they were away from combat, the men always wanted to talk about some kind of problem at home, a problem that usually arrived in the mail—a sick parent, an abusive father, a crazy brother, a pregnant girlfriend, or an unanticipated ex-girlfriend. I had to make the judgment call on who got on the next resupply chopper for a trip to the rear to see the chaplain. It wasn't easy, because no matter how good the men were, there were always a few slackers. But they were all human, and they all had lives back in The World that affected them. In retrospect, it is remarkable that with all the problems at home, these young Marines still put their lives on the line and stayed on mission.

We got relief from the rain by sleeping in sandbagged bunkers instead of poncho hooches. Big Mike and I often sat up late shooting the bull. I couldn't get too familiar with my men, but Mike was my radio and my hooch-mate, and he was a good Marine. We respected each other. Hell, we were stuck with each other. One night I described the sausage sized leech I had taken off my leg. He seemed impressed.

"I never saw one that big, Mr. D. But, hey, did you ever hear about the guy in Lima Company who had a leech crawl up in his dick? He got blocked up with so much piss in him he damn near exploded."

"You told me before, Mike, and everybody else seems to know a guy it happened to."

"No, I know it's true. I heard it from a doc in Lima Company."

"Yeah, well, you hear a lot of things."

Some days there was just nothing to talk about, and there was nowhere to go, and there was nothing to look at but the surrounding world.

Some previous unit had built a crude chute that was used to drop trash off the one-hundred-foot cliff on the south side of the mountain. Environmental cleanliness was not a concern in my war. Over time the trash at the bottom of cliff had grown so large that it could provide the enemy with an avenue of approach. I had the men drop a couple of incendiary grenades in the pile to burn it. Two things went wrong. The wind shifted, bringing the smoke back to us. It smelled simultaneously like burning rubber, paper, clothing, cardboard, rotten fruit, and shit. A couple of the guys puked; it was that bad. The other, more dangerous thing involved ordnance. After the pile had burned for half an hour or so, it started exploding. Four, maybe five sharp explosions had all of us face down on the deck, then we looked over to be sure the explosions came from the garbage and not from some attacking enemy. I don't know what it was, but it was not an attack. Maybe some of the fabled mines, maybe somebody had accidentally dumped some grenades or mortar rounds down the chute. Luckily, the explosions were far enough below us that nobody was injured. Still, it was sobering. We didn't burn anymore.

The little position was overrun with rats. The men mixed C-4 plastic explosive with peanut butter and left it out for the rats. One of them claimed that he knew a guy who knew a guy who had proved the C-4 was poisonous to rats. We found some dead rats after that and assumed the formula worked. I still don't know if it did.

We had been there about a week and had been socked in most of that time, so we weren't getting resupply. We didn't need ammo, and there seemed to be enough food, but water was running low. Mountain streams were everywhere below us, so finding water was not the issue. Getting safely outside the wire was. There was a small opening in the wire on the east side of the hill, with what looked like a path. It was hard to tell. The jungle grew so relentlessly that any unused trail could disappear in a week. Still, it looked like a way out.

I called the squad leaders together and asked for volunteers to try to find a way out and bring back water.

"I'll take it," said Corporal Gregg.

"Okay, gather up as many canteens as your men can carry and take only volunteers. Be careful."

Within thirty minutes, Gregg and his second squad were leaving the perimeter, loaded with canteens. We all held our breath, but the men silently disappeared into the jungle without incident. After about forty-five minutes, Gregg reported he had found a good stream, and an hour later, the squad was safely back. The whole effort was not a big deal, but it would have been much different if someone had stepped on a mine or if they had contact with the enemy. We were all lucky.

The next day was sunny, and the choppers brought us water.

One morning we woke up above the clouds. Thick fog was just below us, and we had the sense of floating on a white sea. We were enveloped by the sky; the stillness was palpable. We could not possibly be involved in a war. Then the peace of the morning was interrupted by the sound of helicopters coming from the west. As they got closer, we could see men hanging on external lines beneath one of the choppers, which came over us and hovered above my tiny wooden LZ. The men on the external lines dropped down. One was dead and had been lashed to his line. They untied him, loaded everyone into the helicopter, and flew away east. They were Americans, but beyond that, they were a mystery. No markings were on the helicopters. They didn't ask permission to land inside my lines, Big Mike couldn't get them to respond on the radio aircraft frequency he had, and they just disappeared. It was obvious the men were a recon team that had been pulled out of a firefight over near the Laotian border or inside Laos. I reported the incident to my company commander but never heard any more about it. The whole episode was surreal.

A few days later, we again woke up above the clouds, little knowing that the rumor about all the mines would soon be proven true. This time two Army Hueys showed up. The fog was so thick at their base that they could not land and were running low on fuel, so they dropped in on me. My LZ was large enough for only one chopper, so the other one landed in a little clearing just down the hill to the west. An Army major jumped off the chopper on my LZ and demanded that I send someone down to protect his other helicopter and crew. It hacked me that he gave the order, much less imperiously demanded protection for his exposed men and equipment. I already had McFarland's squad getting mounted up, so I didn't need his prompting and politely told him so. I also told him that we were surrounded by unmarked minefields and that for all I knew his other Huey had landed in one, which didn't make him happy. I wasn't happy about having to send my guys outside the wire, but an unprotected crew and helicopter were down there.

The squad picked gingerly through the wire and had nearly reached the Huey when one of the men stepped on a mine. I don't know whose mine it was, what kind it was, or how long it had been there, but luckily it had little force and succeeded only in breaking the kid's ankle. But now we had a stranded Huey, an injured Marine, and a rifle squad all in a minefield. My Marines got the wounded man on the Huey and started setting up a perimeter. About twenty minutes had passed when the major got back on his Huey, and both choppers cranked up and took off without so much as a thank you. I guess the pilots found out the fog was lifting wherever they were going, and it was safe to leave, so off they went, taking my Marine. The rest of the squad managed to get back inside our position without further incident. Luckily, that was our only unintended venture outside the wire. I never saw my Marine again. I hoped he was hurt badly enough to go home but not so seriously as to be crippled. They once called that a million-dollar wound.

Still, it galled that the Army bastards left without bothering to thank us for our trouble or acknowledging our loss. We had done the right thing. We had to protect the chopper crew and would have done so without being told to, but a little thanks would have been nice. I never did like majors.

❊ ❊ ❊

In fifty years, I have yet to meet a Vietnam veteran who thought the country was beautiful. They remember the dust and the mud; the jungle and the rice paddies; squalid villages and towns; ancient women and men; naked, dirty children; barbed wire; sandbag bunkers; and at every American installation, half-barrels pulled out from under the ubiquitous privies—shitters in common parlance—with burning kerosene emitting the kind of smoke you never want to smell again. I also saw a lot of ugliness, but looking back on my quiet time on OP 950, the worst details have blurred away.

The good part was the view. Our hilltop was about fifteen miles east of the Laotian border, and we could see into Laos. Nothing was there but mountains and jungle, but it was neat to see into a foreign country, even if the enemy used it as their supply route. Thirty or so miles to the east was the South China Sea. The sea was more blue than the sky, and the beaches were sugar white. The coastal area was patched with rice paddies laid out in endless squares. A few villages were visible among the rice paddies.

The Cam Lo River rose in the mountains to the north and flowed past Quang Tri City near the coast. Farther north and northeast was the DMZ and more jungle. We could catch glimpses of the Ben Hai River, the nominal border between North and South, flowing down the middle of the DMZ to the sea. Beyond the Z was North Vietnam and more jungle. Six-thousand-foot Dong Voi Mep, the mountain we called the Tiger Tooth, hung over us to the north, topping the mountains around it. Its profile above the tree line looked like a perfect feline fang. In an earlier time, the French had called it le Dent du Tigre. It was the only mountain I saw that didn't have jungle on its top.

I cannot forget the distant sea, the beaches, the bright green rice paddies that lay in contrast to the dark green jungle, and the lighter green elephant grass that grew everywhere else. A granite Tiger Tooth rose above the jungle green. Brown roads linked the few visible towns and villages. It was strangely peaceful and quiet. Everything within view, even the moonscape around Khe Sanh, was hauntingly beautiful. I would sit and enjoy the landscape for hours.

So, we stood watch, looked for enemy movement, and enjoyed the scenery until one day the helicopters came and took us off. It was a relatively good gig while it lasted. A week later, we launched into an operation that kept us in contact with the enemy every day for more than two months.

Author on OP 950, January 1969

— 26 —

Dewey Canyon

Operation Dewey Canyon is legendary in the Marine Corps. It launched in January 1969 and ended two months later. The operation is memorable because it was brilliantly executed and because we inflicted terrible injury on the enemy, both in equipment, supplies, and lives. It cost us, too.

A year earlier, in February 1968, the Viet Cong and NVA had launched the Tet offensive, so-called because it happened during Tet, the Vietnamese New Year. Everyone was on holiday routine under an unofficial truce, and the Americans and their allies were caught off guard. It was a surprise attack not unlike the 1944 German offensive from the Ardennes Forest in what came to be known as the Battle of the Bulge. As in Belgium in 1944, the Americans and their allies suffered tremendous early losses, but this time television sets at home showed men fighting and dying in the old Imperial Capital at Hue and on the American Embassy grounds in Saigon. Reporters, who never ventured into the jungle that I saw, observed death and destruction close at hand, and it looked to them like we were losing. But after three weeks of bitter fighting, all lost territory had been retaken, and the enemy forces were all but destroyed, crippling the Viet Cong for years, much as the Americans and British in 1944 destroyed an entire German army.

Unlike the Battle of the Bulge, which was hailed as a great allied victory, the American press treated the Tet offensive as an utter defeat. Since the reporters hanging out in bars in Saigon had probably never seen or heard a battle, it was our bad luck that they saw one that at first went badly. By early 1968, serious opposition to the war had gained the national spotlight, and every setback, however temporary, was branded as a failure.

In the Tet offensive, our troops were initially beaten because they were surprised. They should not have been surprised, but they were not defeated. From a military standpoint, calling Tet a defeat was outrageous; we got hurt, but we slaughtered the enemy in return. But by that time, uninformed politicians running the war were looking over their shoulders and trying to shift the blame. Their strategies turned with the prevailing political wind. The press told them we had lost, and they believed it, as did the people.

A year later, in late '68 and early '69, the NVA were amassing supplies along the Laotian border for a second Tet offensive. The Ninth Marines got the order to interdict the flow of supplies into the South. Dewey Canyon was the operation that made it happen.

We destroyed the better part of two NVA divisions, put something like two thousand NVA dead or wounded out of the war, captured five hundred tons of munitions and weapons, and prevented the planned 1969 Tet offensive. When the operation was over, the CG of XXIV Corps was so impressed by the unit's valor that he nominated the Ninth Marines for a Presidential Unit Citation, later approved. The Ninth Marines became the only Marine unit in Vietnam to receive the Army Presidential Unit Citation. Those who were there thought it was a becoming honor. We paid a hell of a price for it—130 dead, 932 wounded. And every Marine who fought there was changed forever.

Kilo Company was in the thick of it. The entire Ninth Regiment and supporting artillery were lifted into the jungle near the Laotian border in an area where American forces had never ventured. We were fifty miles from our base and totally dependent on helicopters. The enemy was there in force, protecting their supplies. We attacked up the mountains every day, and we were in contact with the enemy every day. "In contact" does not mean we exchanges phone calls.

All we could see was jungle. All we could feel was heat and exhaustion. Any trails we ran across were generally small and would dead end for no obvious reason. If we found a well-used trail, we knew who was using it. Knowing the enemy was in front of us but not knowing exactly when we would make contact, we pressed on.

Dewey Canyon was a relentless fight. Contact was close. The regiment moved with three battalions abreast against a well-entrenched enemy, but there were no open fields, no tanks, jeeps, personnel carriers, or trucks. The jungle was the only presence besides my Marines and the enemy, and the jungle was oppressive. It was everywhere. You might get a glimpse of a nearby hilltop if an artillery shell had cleared out some trees, but you saw little else. Ground navigation was extremely difficult.

Since we were attacking, the NVA chose when and where to stop and dig in. When we met, we had to take them out. Contact typically started when they opened fire as Marines came up the hill. Our only option was to spread out as best we could and take the fight to the enemy. The tactics depended on the terrain and the size of the enemy force. Determining how many enemies were in front of us was difficult, but with time the ear gauged the volume of fire and made reasoned assumptions. Given time, I would call in a fire mission from whatever was available, anything from the company 60 mm mortars to big artillery.

If the force was large, I would take two squads to get on the enemy's flank while the remaining squad kept the enemy entertained with rifle and machine-gun fire. When we got in line on the flank, we would hit them hard. Like every platoon leader, I always led the charge from the center.

If the enemy force was small, we would get on line and charge up the middle. Either way, it was brutal. The entire operation was brutal. Dewey Canyon produced two Medals of Honor, one posthumous.

In early 1971, when antiwar fever in the United States was reaching the boiling point, the so-called Winter Soldier Investigation by the Vietnam Veterans Against the War had show "trials" in which veterans testified about the many war crimes they had participated in or witnessed. It was mostly crap—the self-created killers who got a thrill saying their *mea culpas* on TV (later retracted)—but two members of the Ninth Marines testified truthfully that they had been in Dewey Canyon and that we had actually attacked into Laos. The peaceniks were horrified. Imagine, violating the neutrality of poor little Laos. It was criminal behavior on a world front.

That was also crap. The idea that Laos's "neutrality" was violated is laughable. The NVA were there, had been there for years, and Laos did nothing about it—could do nothing about it—so the NVA used Laos as their transportation route and staging area. The Ho Chi Minh Trail was a camouflaged superhighway that allowed the enemy to bring men and supplies through Laos, but I don't recall ever hearing any of the antiwar protesters back home complain about that little international border violation.

One of our companies did intentionally venture into Laos during Dewey Canyon, across a line on a map that on the ground looked like just more jungle, and successfully ambushed a convoy of NVA carrying munitions intended for use against Americans and our allies farther south. They killed a lot of enemy, too. So, they went into Laos. We should have done it regularly. If we had been allowed to go where it was forbidden, where the enemy was hiding, we might have won the damn war.

It's one thing to hold to your principles and observe the international law against crossing borders. It's another thing to sacrifice your children while doing so. Now it appears we're doing the same thing in the Middle East with the notable exception of taking out Bin Laden. And Bin Laden was holed up in a populated area. The NVA was operating in a jungle. Laos would never have known if we had launched a major battle across the border, but of course the American press would have told the world, bringing our grievous sin to the light of day.

The press killed a lot of our kids in their search for truth. God, how I hated them.

— 27 —

TMI

Newly commissioned Marine lieutenants go through a six-month course of training at the Basic School at Quantico, Virginia. In 1968 it was five months. Perhaps the war required cannon fodder sooner rather than later, so the training was speeded up. I raised some eyebrows in the Basic School when my turn came to give a practice demonstration for the course called TMI—the Technique of Military Instruction. The course name reminded me of the old saw about the Holy Roman Empire, which was neither holy, nor Roman, nor an empire.

When I gave my presentation, I talked about the Vietnamese people, a people who wanted a unified country under a democratic government, with food, jobs, freedom of movement, and freedom from domination by foreign powers. Everyone liked the patriotic propaganda until I disclosed that the content of my lecture and the description of the peoples' desires came from captured Viet Cong literature. There were hushed murmurs from my classmates about sympathizing with the enemy, not all of it in jest.

The instructor, whose opinion mattered, wondered out loud if I had what it would take to be a leader of Marines. He resisted my explanation that if you don't know your enemy you can't effectively fight him and that as best I could tell the home-grown Viet Cong actually believed they were fighting for their idea of freedom, however misplaced their belief might be. The North Vietnamese really believed they were trying to free their brothers in the South. In other words, they were not just mindless communist pawns.

You underestimate your enemy's motivation at your peril, a lesson that still seems to elude us. It also defeated us in Vietnam. The North Vietnamese and the Viet Cong were serious about winning and took the pain longer than we were willing to. Our leaders should have anticipated that.

It didn't matter. The idea that the conflict in Vietnam really was a civil war was anathema within the military, then and now. Yes, the Russians and the Chinese were pushing to bring the enlightened benefits of communism to the entire world. There was indeed a Cold War. We in the West knew that communism was not democracy, much less enlightened democracy. Communism allowed little freedom, but that did not mean the average Viet Cong or the NVA agreed with us. So, roughly a year after I got an unfavorable grade in the TMI class for seeming to favor the enemy, I felt sorry for a dead NVA soldier—or his family, I wasn't sure which—who had tried to kill my Marines, and I hated him at the same time. I did not and do not see the two feelings as mutually exclusive.

—28—

The Beast

In February 1969, about three weeks into Operation Dewey Canyon, I was following the lead squad of the thirty or so Marines of my badly depleted platoon, grunting our way up a trail on yet another jungle hill. My first squad was in front. Second and third squads were behind me. We were in single file with flanks out. The jungle was no place to march in formation, or even to form a line of battle.

It was late afternoon. We had been on patrol all day, and we were tired. It was miserably hot, but at least it had quit raining. We had crossed all our checkpoints and were headed toward the company position.

We had not seen any enemy all day. But months of doing the same thing over and over again had keened my senses somehow, and I knew that enemy were close by, even though nothing was visible beyond the immediate ten feet or so allowed by a thick, triple-canopy jungle.

"Handset, Mike."

Big Mike handed me the handset of the PRC-25 radio he carried. Marines predictably called it the PRICK-25.

I called the squad leader in front of me.

"Kilo three alpha, Kilo three."

"Three alpha."

"I smell something. Slow down. We're getting too strung out. And don't let your point get so far ahead you can't support him."

I didn't need to remind him, but I did anyway. Caution was something we knew was necessary but sometimes forgot, particularly late in the day when we were on our way back to the company. Walking an old trail in the jungle does not get easier as the hours pass, particularly for the guys humping the machine guns and ammo. We tried to be stealthy, but that was impossible. Besides, we didn't hide well. The enemy saw the helicopters dropping us in and resupplying us, and we stunk of body odor, cigarettes, and insect repellant.

"Roger that, three."

"Three out."

"You really think there's gooks up there, Mr. D? It's been quiet today."

Big Mike was worried. Concern was in his voice, even fear, which was unusual. He more than lived up to his nickname; he looked like a linebacker but with a babyface. He was nineteen and unmarried, but the only thing he ever told me he worried about was losing his girlfriend. Like most Marines, he accepted the fact that we faced danger every day. I couldn't convincingly reassure him, though.

"We've had contact almost every day for a month," I said, "and we're getting closer to their supply base. They'll let us know when we find them."

Finding them was euphemistically called a point contact, meaning the NVA hid in fighting holes or bunkers somewhere along the trail, usually near the crest of a hill, and opened up when our point man got close enough for them to hear us, even if the thick jungle prevented them from seeing us. Usually, we didn't know they were there until the shooting started. Sometimes we were lucky and saw them first and could back off and call for artillery.

※ ※ ※

The night before, Big Mike and I sat miserably in the mud in our makeshift hooch, wishing it would stop raining, Mike told me he didn't like the way things were going. We were taking a lot of casualties, mostly wounded, but some of the guys had been killed.

That morning word had gotten back to us that Preacher was dead. Preacher, a private first class from somewhere in Georgia, was a rifleman in third squad. He felt The Call to hold a country version of divine services on Sunday mornings, circumstances permitting. Most of the guys attended when they could. Everybody loved Preacher. He performed a needed service because if there were chaplains in the jungle, I never saw one.

Preacher had taken a bullet in the butt three days earlier. The last time we saw him, he was grinning his big hick grin and waving at us as he walked up the ramp of a medevac helicopter. The guys were hooting at him about being shot in the ass while saying they hoped he had the million-dollar wound that would take him out of the war. By the time the chopper got to the field hospital, he was dead. That's all we ever heard.

Big Mike was a regular at Preacher's services and was devastated by his death.

"If Preacher got it, we're all in some bad shit, Mr. D. I think God is mad at us. Why else would he take Preacher?"

The news of Preacher's death shook me too, but not necessarily for the theological implications. I wondered at the chances. Why would what looked like a million-dollar wound do more than just take Preacher out of the war?

"I don't know, Mike." My boot made a sucking sound as I pulled it out of the mud.

"We're part of a big operation. The whole regiment is attacking up into the mountains where the enemy's main supply base is. We're being told it's going well. It may be going well for the brass, but for us grunts on the front line, a death—too many deaths—is not what we would call doing well. If we lose one man, it's a lousy day. At division, it's a good day if the operation costs only a dozen or so Marines."

"You mean they don't care?"

"Of course they care. They don't want dead Marines, but they do want us to kill the enemy and get his supplies. And to them it isn't personal like it is to us. They didn't know Preacher or any of the other kids we've lost. Whether the operation is going well is a matter of perspective."

Thus it has always been. At the Battle of Concord and Lexington, a ragtag, loosely trained group of Minutemen won a remarkable and surprising victory over more than seven hundred British regulars. The battle has been remembered in slogan and verse (Emerson's "Concord Hymn" with "the shot heard 'round the world," and Longfellow's "Paul Revere's Ride"), and is celebrated both as the first battle of the Revolution and a great victory for the colonists. Yet forty-nine colonists died in that battle. Their victory, and that of their families and loved ones, was neither positive nor great. In battle, the guys at the front take the casualties. Victories are won, but the victory always goes to the living, not the dead.

"Anyway, I got a bad feeling," said Mike.

Mike worked on changing the radio's battery without getting mud on the contacts, but the mud won.

"And we're up shit's creek," he griped, "if I can't even keep the radio clean."

"We'll get through this, Mike. We always do."

"Is that a promise?"

"My word of honor, Marine."

※ ※ ※

I quit thinking about Big Mike and Preacher and the odds of dying and tried to concentrate on the present. Our patrol was almost over, but almost is a relative term. We all felt the mental effect of physical exhaustion. And even though I had a vague sense of danger, I caught myself thinking about how good it would feel to get my boots off and sit for a while.

Without warning, the screaming whip of machine-gun tracers split the air from in front of me. The bullets went over my head as I hit the deck. Big Mike took the entire burst in his neck. As I scrambled to my feet, I turned and was horror-struck to see what was left of Mike. He had been hit in the neck so many times that in an instant, his head was separated from his body. His head was hanging from a flap of skin below his left ear. His eyes were open, and his teeth showed a lop-sided upside-down grin. The machine gun had done the grisly work of a band saw.

One second Mike was walking behind me as he always had; the next second he was falling, headless, toward me. The big man's heart seemed to give one last beat as he fell. The full force of his heart's final contraction erupted from his now exposed carotid arteries and showered my face and chest with blood. I jumped back on reflex, seeing but not believing.

My world imploded. My mind went numb for a second, but adrenalin quickly took over. I picked up Mike's M-16 and yelled for the men behind me to follow as I sprinted up the hill. In an instant, I spotted a man in a primitive bunker off to one side of the trail. He had let the first squad go by before opening the firing slit in his bunker so he could get a shot at an officer, meaning me. He was pounding on his machine gun with his fist. It had jammed during the burst that hit Mike.

That gave me the precious few seconds I needed. I was twenty feet away by then, still running and completely on fire. I screamed as I switched Mike's M-16 to fully automatic.

"You bastard! You fucking gook bastard!"

I emptied an entire magazine into his face from a maybe three feet. His head disintegrated into a gory cloud of vaporized bone, brain tissue, hair, skin, and blood.

I yelled for another magazine because I didn't carry a rifle and had no ammo for one. Little, by then right beside me, grabbed my arm.

"I think you got this one, Lieutenant. You don't need any more ammo."

I reached for the K-Bar knife on my belt.

"He killed Mike! I'll cut his fucking throat!"

"He doesn't have a throat. You blew it away. You've done enough. It's over."

But I hadn't done enough, and it wasn't over. The man's head was a lousy trade for Mike's.

Dear God, I thought, *how could this happen?* But I knew. The bastard was aiming at me while I was daydreaming about getting some rest. I felt a twinge of guilt—guilt because I had been daydreaming, which did not affect anything, and guilt because Mike had been massacred in my place.

And Mike and I had talked about Preacher the night before. That brought bad luck. Mike had been right. Things were not going well.

— 29 —

Vengeance

In the breathless seconds that followed, I tried to take in what was going on around me, but suddenly everything stopped. I just stood there numb, unmoving. Bone fragments and brain tissue were on my boots. I looked like I was the casualty, and emotionally maybe I was. I had a real casualty to deal with, but I couldn't do anything. I wanted to vomit, but nothing came up.

"You okay, Lieutenant?" asked Little.

"Yeah, give me a minute."

"Take your time. The rest of the bastards ran. You scared them shitless."

I thought for a long time, taking in what Little had said, then asked, "How many were there?"

"Looks like five or six got away. The headless horseman isn't going anywhere." Little's attempt at humor was not appreciated, but I didn't say anything.

Little called for medevac and put the platoon on defense until the helicopter came for Mike. I did nothing.

I was the platoon leader, and I needed to be in charge, but I was somewhere else, somewhere I shouldn't have been. For the second time in five or six months, I had killed a man. My shock and anger at Mike's death had momentarily overwhelmed me, and I blew the man away with a savagery I didn't know I had in me. I had killed with murderous intent. And I had not wanted just to kill this man for killing Mike. I had wanted to annihilate him, to rob him of his very soul. It was over the top, but my God, it felt good. It was so good that for those two seconds I was on a natural high, the highest high. The highest two seconds of my life.

And now the killing was over, and there was time to think. I was baffled by the enormity of it—whatever it was. Maybe animal reaction, or adrenalin, testosterone, anger, fear, whatever. I didn't like it. Was this war turning me from a thoughtful, rarely profane, intelligent, and insightful Marine officer into just another mindless killer? And if it happened to me, were my men experiencing the same thing? But my killing the guy who slaughtered Mike was not the problem now. The problem was leadership. Leadership required a leader while I just stood there, blanked. I couldn't do anything. It was the classic freeze-up. Had I come this far just to go berserk and lose control of myself in front of the men who trusted me, simply because of one more casualty?

But this wasn't just one more casualty. Big Mike was my radio. He followed me everywhere. We had lived together for six months. At night we talked about football, or friends, or cars, or laughed at stories like the one about the guy with a leech up his dick, which wasn't funny if it was true. We never talked about anything too personal because of our difference in rank, but deep inside, I knew that Mike was the closest thing to a friend I had in this goddamned shithole of a world.

Now Mike's life had been traded for this gook. We would hunt down the others, but for now, the score was one each. A life for a life. What a goddamn shame. My mind was a deep dark hole, and I couldn't see out of it.

One of my squad leaders touched my shoulder.

"That was for Mike, Mr. D. What you did came from all of us. Just cool out for a minute. It's okay. We got your back, sir."

From behind me, one of the men whispered, "Fuckin' A, Lieutenant, Fuckin' A." The language of affirmation. They sensed what I was feeling. I relaxed a little. There was nothing more to say, nothing more to do but wait for the medevac.

The men put Mike on a stretcher and loaded it on the chopper. I couldn't watch. I tried to wipe what I thought was sweat off my face but discovered it was blood, and it wasn't coming off. *Just like Lady Macbeth,* I thought, *and murder most foul. No, she couldn't get the blood off her hands, but the murder line was from Hamlet.* I searched my memory but couldn't call up the verse: "Murder most foul, as in the best it is, but this most foul, strange, and unnatural." That was how Mike was murdered, strangely and unnaturally. *Christ, I'm in the middle of a war, and I'm thinking about Shakespeare. I must be going crazy.* Finally, I got out a canteen, sat down, and washed my face as best I could. *Dear God, Mike. Dear God, dear God, dear God. What next? What else?*

The chopper flew away. I sat there trying to force my brain to click back in, to steel up.

For God's sake, don't just sit there; get off your ass. You can grieve later. Mike is dead. He isn't coming back. Your job now is to protect

*your men and kill the bastards. So, you killed one, now go kill some
more. This is war; this is the game. You're not in the game if you're
not playing—if you're not killing.*

I had to do something besides kill one gook. Leaning on
Mike's rifle, I pushed myself to my feet. I took a deep breath.

"Call up the squad leaders, Sergeant Little. It's time to
get even. We're going hunting. And get me some rifle ammo."

"Aye, sir." Little grinned.

Somebody whispered, "Fuckin' A, Mr. D."

I felt a tremendous sense of relief. I had a job to do, and I
knew how to do it. I figured the gooks that ran would set up
another ambush on the next hill. I called for artillery to prep
the hill. I would split my force to set a trap. Little gathered
the squad and section leaders.

"All right, men, listen up. The hill we are on is 595 meters
high. Five or six NVA fled this hill and are probably waiting
for us on Hill 610, the next hill, 150 meters to our east. We
will set up an ambush on the trail on the other side of Hill 610.
Sergeant Williams, you will take your squad and move in an
arc to our left around to the other side of the Hill 610 and set
up the ambush. The machine-gun section will go with you. You
must be absolutely quiet. If the enemy hears you, the ambush is
blown. Second and third squads will move with me to the right
and get on line roughly one hundred meters from the gooks.

Lance Corporal Jones, you and your rocket section plus
one fire team from third squad will remain here. Corporal
McFarland, who leads your strongest fire team?"

"Preacher did, sir, so it will be Jamison."

"Okay, Jamison, your team will stay here with rockets.
You are senior, so you will be in command of the detachment
staying here."

Jamison swelled almost imperceptibly. "Aye, sir."

"Jones, you're clear on that?"

"Yes, sir. Jamie's in charge."

"Roger, that. Now, you men will make noise so the gooks will think we're still here. Normal noise, not a lot of fake stuff. Maintain your perimeter in case any gooks show up. You will be on your own for thirty minutes or so. I will call you when you can join us.

"When first squad is ready, second and third will charge by fire and maneuver up the south side of the hill, all weapons firing. Hopefully, the gooks will run, and first squad will wipe them out. Sergeant Williams, when you are in place, the word to go is 'Set.' Any questions?"

No one said anything. I read their faces. They were ready to rock.

"All right, we'll move out when arty has finished. Check your weapons and ammo."

Fox Battery, Second Battalion, Twelfth Marines, was our regiment's direct support battery. Fox was at a fire support base a couple of miles northwest of us. Over the next ten or fifteen minutes, they unerringly dropped thirty or so 105 mm rounds on Hill 610 while we tried to melt into the ground in case there was a short round. Short rounds were rare, but they happened. Nobody wanted to die by friendly fire.

You would think nobody could live through the kind of bombardment Fox laid on Hill 610, but Marines had learned otherwise on Peleliu and Iwo Jima during World War II, where the Japanese were well dug in. If the gooks had been digging in while we were dealing with Mike's body, or if they had prepared positions in advance, they would likely still be there. Either way, we were going for it.

I knew that dividing my force in the face of the enemy was against military doctrine, especially a platoon dividing into three parts. If this little maneuver failed, if the small group left behind got hit hard, if some Marines got killed, I would likely be relieved, if not sent before a court-martial. I didn't care. I was Lee and Jackson at Chancellorsville. I was the hammer against the anvil. I was unstoppable. I was pissed.

When the artillery barrage ended, my Marines did exactly as ordered. The rockets and fire team we left behind sounded like a platoon settling in for the night. I got my two squads in position. A little ravine ran parallel to the south side of Hill 610. It gave us good cover. After what seemed an eternity, Williams led his man around the north side of the hill and had them in place for the ambush. He whispered, "Set," into his radio. Time to go.

I led my group, all of us on line, charging and yelling toward the gooks' flank with every weapon firing. The trick worked. The five remaining gooks took a few ineffective shots at us, then retreated down the back of the hill. They were slaughtered by Williams's waiting squad and machine guns. I didn't ask how many rounds it took to kill those five men, but what I heard as the ambush was triggered sounded refreshingly, delightfully, violent.

Six to one now, you gook bastards. It wasn't enough, but it was a start. There would be more.

The men we left behind joined us. They reported no enemy activity. We went down the east slope of Hill 610 and joined Sergeant Williams. He and his men were pleased with themselves.

"Worked like a charm, Mr. D."

"You guys did great," I said. Then addressing the squad leaders: "Okay, people, let's get a move on. Time to get back."

"Don't you want these gooks buried, Lieutenant?" asked Little.

I think Little was half joking, but after the weirdness about the kid in the hole, I guess he had to ask.

I didn't even pause to think. "Let the maggots eat them. For all I care, they can rot here; then they can rot in hell."

— 30 —

Doubt

I briefed the Skipper when we got back to the company—a fairly routine report: one KIA, six enemy bodies. I described our ambush of the NVA after the initial contact, after they killed Mike. The Skipper said that it sounded like I had handled it well and that he was sorry about Mike. I glossed over the bad part—my loss of control. I said nothing about jackhammering the gook's face.

I went to check the platoon's part of the perimeter. The men were subdued. They had given more than they got, but they were still shaken by Mike's death, by the way he had died, by what they had seen. I overheard one say that the lieutenant had butchered that gook so bad his mama wouldn't recognize him. The men around him laughed.

So that's how I will be remembered, I thought. *The butcher. It could be worse. At least they weren't talking about my behavior when I had let my emotions get the better of me.*

I went back to my hooch. *Damn*, I thought. *Damn*. Big

Mike was a good man. Everybody liked him. He didn't have to stand lines, but he was up half the night following me around when I checked the perimeter. He never had to walk point, but the other men didn't envy him because, as a radio, Mike was always a target. The enemy knew the radio antennas followed the officers, and they tried first to kill us. The gook with the machine gun missed me but got Mike. Mike was an especially big target, and in the end, his size killed him. If he had been six inches shorter, he would still have his head. *God, that is macabre thinking.*

I couldn't stop thinking about him. He was from Oklahoma. He had a southern drawl that was more pronounced than those of my Georgia and North Carolina kin. He was twenty, had been in the Corps for two years or so, and stood a couple inches better than six feet, hence the nickname. Mike was more the gentle giant type than the killer Marine, but he knew his business and kept his radio working.

Mike was also a short-timer; he would rotate home in three months. If I could clear it with the Skipper, I would get him a make-work job in the rear during his last month in country. I tried to get short-timers a break if I could. Sometimes we were short of manpower and needed every man we had. When this operation was over, we would get new people, and I would do what I could for Mike.

But all that was now irrelevant. As Mike had said the night before he died, this operation was costing us, and I didn't much like the way it was going either. Preacher wasn't the only kid I had lost, and you never knew who was going to get it next.

Mike died less than two months shy of his twenty-first birthday. *What a goddamn shame.* That happened to a lot of guys, guys who were even younger and had less time left in country than Mike, but this was personal. This was about Big Mike. Now he would be missed. I would miss him the most. I felt incredibly sad.

I also felt remorse, but not over Mike's death. The remorse, the regret, even the shame I felt was over my loss of control. I had just frozen up, and that is the ultimate failure in leadership. The situation had worked out well, but what if the enemy had started attacking while I stood there in a daze? I wanted to think I would have taken charge, but now there was no way of knowing what would have happened.

The guys seemed to have understood, though. Maybe it was no big deal. Still, I felt like the green second lieutenant every Marine fears—the one who becomes paralyzed under pressure and can't or won't lead. These Marines had to depend on their leaders, and now they had the right to fear that I might fail them again when it mattered more. I had wanted only to be a good officer, to lead troops in battle effectively, and to save as many of their lives as I could. This shitty war was not something I had asked for, but I had to do my part.

Self-doubt can be a destroyer, and it was working on me.

— 31 —

Reward

I was still thinking about Mike and the aftermath of his death when Steve Sax, the lieutenant from second platoon, stuck his head in my hooch. He said he had seen Little talking to the Skipper and wondered if something was up. I just shrugged. I figured Little was telling the Skipper about my loss of control. He probably was.

Little was a lifer and understood that a platoon leader out of control endangered the whole platoon. It was his responsibility to report what he had seen, and I would never criticize him for it if he did, even if it led to my undoing. I thought maybe I would ask Little about it but decided not to. Whatever was going to happen would happen. If I got relieved, I would be sent to some command bunker to spend the rest of my tour monitoring radios all night. They probably wouldn't court-martial me because I didn't get anyone killed.

I couldn't stand the thought of being relieved of my command, though. I loved these brave men too much. I had let them down momentarily, but no harm had come from it. I hoped they understood. I just didn't want to think about it. I didn't want to think about anything. I made myself start thinking about replacing Mike. The thought that this could also disgrace me in my father's eyes did not occur to me right then.

The next morning, we were saddling up for a patrol. My concentration was shot. I felt like I had no business taking these men into the jungle again. I couldn't bear the thought of letting my men down. Indecision could kill, and I was up to my ass in it right then.

Finally, I decided I had to quit agonizing and talk to Little.

"Sergeant Little," I said, "tell me about what happened when Mike was killed."

"What do you mean, sir?"

"I don't know," I said. "I know I killed the gook. Then I don't remember anything for a long time, like I was out of it or something. Did I blow it?"

His eyes narrowed. He looked at me for what seemed like forever. Then he smiled, then chuckled, then laughed.

"No way, Lieutenant," he said. "If you were out of it, it wasn't for long. You were taking a breather, that's all," he said. "Five, maybe ten seconds. Besides, if the gooks had attacked, you would have had us on line and charging into them. We got faith in you, Lieutenant."

"Little, be straight with me. This isn't funny."

"Not funny, sir. I wasn't laughing at you. It's just ... well, I never saw an officer do what you did. If I'd blown that gook's head off, I would have puked. Hell, I told the Skipper you should get a medal. He said he might write you up."

I didn't know what to think, so I tried to put it out of my head. There was still a war to fight. I needed to get back to being a Marine. A medal. Ha. No way for that little screwup.

A year later, I was informed that I was being awarded a Bronze Star with the "V" device. A year after that, when I was no longer on active duty, I received it in the mail. By then, I had moved on. The medal went in a drawer. I didn't want it anyway. I wanted Mike to be alive.

Mike's family got a Purple Heart. The only thing Mike got was his name inscribed on a wall.

— 32 —

Terror

The company moved out of its overnight position early in the morning. Third platoon brought up the rear. Today would be like the rest. We had gone no more than a hundred meters when we started taking fire from the right. I couldn't see where the fire was coming from. I started getting my men to face right and go after whoever was out there when something hit my left hand, knocking my compass to the ground. A bullet had entered the soft flesh of my palm nearest the little finger and come out on the other side. Blood spurted like a fountain, and my little finger curled up upon itself. I didn't feel pain, just surprise. I looked down, trying to locate my compass. Without my compass, I was incomplete. It had been knocked about a meter to my left. As I reached for it, I realized that I was covering it with blood.

Little was suddenly behind me.

"You okay, Mr. D?"

"I'll live."

I took the field dressing from its pack on my web belt and wrapped it around my hand to stop the bleeding. By then, the men in second squad had chased off the NVA that had been firing at us.

Suddenly I heard shots from down the hill, from the front of the column. It sounded like a major point contact. The column stalled. The radios were full of traffic, but I couldn't tell what was happening. Whatever it was, first and second platoons and the Skipper were near the action, so I could do nothing but have my men face out and watch for enemy on our flank. After thirty minutes or so, the shooting died down. The column started moving. I called the Skipper to tell him I was hit.

"This is six. How bad?"

"Flesh wound, bullet through the soft part of the base of my left hand."

"Go back to our old position. I'll call for medevac."

We had left a squad from second platoon on the previous night's position to wait for choppers to pick up two ambulatory casualties.

"I'm okay," I said. "I'll go when the day's fighting is over."

"Do as you're told."

"Roger."

"Six out."

I gave my map to Little.

"You have to take it from here. I'm sure I'll be back soon. They just need to sew me up. Good luck."

"We'll be waiting for you, Mr. D."

I turned and started back up the trail we had come down. As I passed the men behind me, they wished me luck. Two squads plus machine guns and rockets were behind me, so the line was long. When I reached the end of the column, I realized that the last man was out of the old position, and I would have to cross fifty meters of no-man's land on a jungle path to get back to the detached squad on the hill. I had no idea whether there were now enemy between me and the squad, and I had no radio. I turned back to the tail of the column only to see that they had moved on down the hill. I was alone. I drew my .45 and sprinted up the hill. When I reached the clearing, I saw the squad in a small defensive perimeter.

"Don't shoot!" I yelled as I ran at them. I didn't need to be killed by friendly fire.

I sat down to wait for the chopper that was already on the way for the two casualties. Now there would be three. Nobody said anything. There was still some firing below us at the head of the column, and everybody looked a little grim. Daily contact with the enemy was beginning to wear on all of us.

In about fifteen minutes, a CH-46 hovered into position and landed in our little LZ. I helped the two other Marines up the ramp and sat down. The chopper leaped off the ground and gained altitude. The pilot obviously knew there were enemy in the area.

I knew north from south, and as we lifted off, I could see we were turning and not heading north toward Charlie Med, our supporting medical detachment, but in the opposite direction.

We started circling over a nearby ridgeline. I guessed that another unit was in contact with the enemy and taking casualties. The chopper would get down and get them out. I was right. Another company was fighting in a saddle, where mountains come down to a connecting ridge, then fall off on either side of the ridge, creating the shape of a saddle. With no cleared landing zone, the pilot had to drop down and hover just above the treetops while the crew chief lowered a horse collar through a hatch in the deck. Three Marines were brought up, two in extremely bad shape. This was a resupply chopper, so no corpsman was on board. We would all have to survive the thirty-minute flight to Charlie Med.

I have never been hit by lightning, but I think I felt something like it when the helicopter was suddenly jolted by a tremendous explosion. From where I sat, its aluminum skin suddenly looked like Swiss cheese. A mortar round apparently hit a tree just below, blowing shrapnel and a shock wave right through us. The chopper lurched and fell to the left, down the side of the saddle. Somehow the pilot regained control, and, by some miracle, we were still flying. The pilot headed north toward Fire Support Base Cunningham and friendlies, about five miles away.

A cold emptiness tightened in my belly when I saw fuel pouring down into the chopper from beneath the rear engine. The crew chief ran back with a tiny fire extinguisher and stood watching jet fuel pour onto the deck. I had been through my share of close calls, including the near miss by a mortar round, if that's what it was, but now it looked like my good luck chips were all in. The helicopter was being tossed around like it had been hit by a tornado. The engines were screaming. Now I felt real fear. I looked down at the field bandage on my hand, pondering the irony. I had been shot through my left hand. The wound was minor considering what it could have been, yet I was surely about to die.

Nobody moved. Nobody said anything. The rear engine

screamed like a banshee. The rotors seemed to be off somehow because they sounded more like flip-flop then the usual whop-whop. To say I was terrified would be a colossal understatement.

They say your entire life will flash before your eyes when you know you are about to die. Mine didn't; there was only the present. All these years later, I can't find adequate words to describe what I felt. I was in mental overload because every thought in my brain popped up simultaneously, each trying to out-shout the others: *Are we going out in a ball of fire like in the movies?—or will we crash in flames, or simply crash in the jungle with NVA around?—the pilot can get to Cunningham if the bird flies and doesn't blow up—we are going down—bad luck—I can't believe this is happening—but the bird is still flying—still more fuel—now getting soaked by fuel. Fear, more fear, indescribable mental pain, the fear of burning, burning to death—the inability to breathe, the lives on the chopper, nine souls, three crew and six grunts all going down—if this is it, this is it—I hope it's instantaneous and painless—why are the engines still running with all that fuel pouring out, pooling around our feet?*

The always noisy engines screeched louder, louder, ever louder, the rear engine most of all. *When will a spark light off all this fuel? This is what I get for being in the wrong place at the wrong time, a bullet through the hand, and I'm dead.*

Joshua made the sun stand still, and I know what it felt like. Time stopped. I saw Death in person, slowly approaching, walking toward me, the empty black sleeve holding a torch, deftly reaching out to light the fire. *I'm hallucinating.* Then again, the screaming engines—the fuel—the realization—disbelief—anger—sorrow—acceptance—*steel yourself for it—shit, this is it—this is really it—this is really it—dear God.*

The engines went silent. The helicopter dropped from several hundred feet, auto-rotating onto an LZ at Cunningham with a loud crunch. Pain stabbed my low back, but I didn't wait around to find out why. I expected an explosion at any second. Several of us dragged the seriously injured Marines far enough from the helicopter to feel safe. We turned, waiting for the helicopter to blow, but the thing just sat there like a squat, menacing, angry insect. I walked off toward some trees and vomited.

The helicopter was still there an hour later when another helicopter picked us up and took us to the field hospital.

Maybe five minutes had elapsed, probably fewer, from the time the helicopter was hit until everyone was safely off.

I regret that I never got a chance to thank the Marine aircrew flying that bird. I still feel guilty. I owe them my life; I owe them everything.

I did not sleep well for a very, very long time.

I saw a psychologist in courtroom TV drama not long ago, testifying in a lawsuit, describing what passengers must feel when they know their airplane is going down. He made it sound terrifying. He didn't have a clue.

— 33 —

War's End

I participated in seven named operations. One was little different from any other. The individual firefights were pretty much the same. The story of Mike's death is not untypical, other than the personal effect it had on me. We humped the hills, counted bodies, dug in, stood to, patrolled, fought, killed, and died or were wounded. We ambushed and got ambushed. I called in airstrikes and artillery. I did my best to take care of my men, but where we went, and when, came from higher up the chain of command. We would take a hill, not to occupy it but to kill whoever held it, then on to the next hill. The repetition was mind-numbing. The fear just made it worse. After a while, there was no sense of accomplishment. It was too dangerous to be called boring, but in a sense, it was.

Dewey Canyon was different to a degree because there we attacked a major force, inflicted great casualties, and captured a tremendous amount of supplies intended for Tet '69, which didn't happen. We kept the NVA away from the populated areas, but I'm not sure the small area we were protecting was their objective. In the end, I don't know that we did much but suffer and cause suffering.

I had been hit twice, once along the Da Krong River (since renamed the Thach Han) back in November '68, and now I had been shot through the hand, and the helicopter crash fractured a vertebra in my low back. None of my wounds were severe or life-threatening, but they were honestly earned. The three injuries got me out of the jungle. I never went back. I still feel guilty about leaving my Marines.

After I left the jungle, I spent about a month recuperating from my gunshot wound and the compression fracture in my spine. The wound was no big deal. The only real treatment for the fracture was bed rest, so rather than let me lie around in the hospital, the CG assigned me to the staff of his assistant division commander with orders to write a report on Operation Dewey Canyon. The ADC's headquarters were at VCB, so I shuffled around interviewing the unit commanders for their input. When I wasn't researching or writing, I was lying in pain on a cot in a tent.

Word got around that I didn't seem to be doing anything, and I guess those that didn't know what I was doing assumed that I had a cushy job or no job at all. I did have a cushy job, but you can't say I hadn't paid my dues for it, and anyway I was in no condition to go back to the bush. So, one day while I was leaving what passed for a mess hall, a major I didn't know stopped me.

"It must be nice being the general's son," he said.

"Yes, sir."

My back hurt like hell, but there was nothing I could say. I found out later that the major was a supply officer, out visiting VCB from the rear. The closest he ever came to combat was stabbing himself with a pencil. He didn't know anything about me, and I wasn't going to satisfy his curiosity.

I told my dad about it years later, after he had retired. He said I should have told him at the time, and he would have done something. I reminded him that there were no favors asked or given. He just smiled. Besides, if I had called the wrath of the Old Man down on some major, it would have just made an enemy out of a superior officer that I surely would run into again. The Marine Corps is a small organization, particularly in the officer corps.

Dad left Vietnam a month before I did. As he boarded his helicopter, he shook my hand and said, "You have proven yourself in combat, Lieutenant." I think he was more proud of me than I was of myself. I didn't think so much of having proven myself as having survived.

I left the Marine Corps when my three-year commitment was up. I knew there would always be those who looked on me as the favored one whose way up was greased by his father and his father's friends, regardless of effort. More critically, I knew I could never live up to what my father had done, no matter how hard I tried. I was aware that George Patton's son retired as a two-star general and was considered by some to be a failure because he was not George Patton. My father retired with four stars and was a world-class hero. He always told me to choose my own career path and do the best I could in it, and it was obvious to me that my career path was not meant to be in the Marine Corps.

I love the Corps and am proud to have been a part of it when it mattered. And while I chose another career path, I am still a Marine. I will always be a Marine.

—34—

Memories

They say odors are triggers that stay with you for a lifetime. I think of Vietnam when I smell insect repellant. It reminds me of mosquitoes the size of helicopters and the malaria against which we took a little pill every day and a big pill every Sunday. Men got malaria anyway and sometimes died from it.

A few years ago, I thought of Vietnam when a hurricane wiped out two dozen trees in my backyard. The smell of eastern red cedars newly split open was much like the smell of the huge mahogany trees our combat engineers would blow apart to clear a landing zone.

There were other odors—blood, gun smoke, the rotting flesh of dead enemy, body odor, gun grease, cigarette smoke, canvas, urine, the jungle, the heat tabs used to warm up C-rations, dysentery-induced diarrhea, earth, vomit, rain, mud, dust, and most of all, fear. You wouldn't think you could smell fear, and you can't describe it when you do, but once you have smelled it, there is no mistaking it. The men I served with were incredibly brave and dedicated, and none of us acknowledged our fear, but it was always there.

I also remember sounds: the ubiquitous helicopters, and gunfire, and the screams of the wounded, the screams of the living, the silence of the dead, shouted orders, the far-off pop of a mortar tube that meant incoming was on the way, and the crack of artillery shells exploding nearby, a noise so incredibly sharp and loud it cut to the marrow—the noise of combat.

On quiet nights, the men talked about their girlfriends or wives, their mothers, and their cars. They rarely talked about their day, or the day before, or the day yet to come. Mostly they talked about their time left in country, and their plans on returning to The World, even though talking about surviving might bring bad luck. Superstitions could be ignored as the situation demanded.

"Mr. D," one told me, "in two weeks, I'll be walking down a grocery store aisle picking what I want off the shelf. I'll be thinking of all you guys."

I was sitting beside a rain-filled fighting hole, stinking of sweat, exhausted, trying to raise the company commander on a balky PRC-25 radio, and wondering what the next hour might bring. This kid's going home was not what I wanted to hear about. I couldn't blame him, though. At least he was one of the ones who made it. I looked forward to buying some groceries of my own one day. I wished him the best and thanked him for remembering us. Seemed silly, but it was heartfelt.

Many nights when things were relatively quiet the Black men in my platoon quietly sang "Joshua Fit the Battle of Jericho." They harmonized like they had been together forever. The words and the tune still haunt me. Not all those wonderful singers made it home, and I still grieve for them.

The late '60s was the era of emerging black power in the United States, but many were fighting against it. Dr. King died for the movement. I admired my Black Marines for even being in the war—for volunteering to fight for a country that mistreated them. Some said they volunteered to avoid being drafted into the Army, but that was lame. An Army soldier had about a 25 percent chance of going to Vietnam. Almost all Marines went.

I know racial strife existed in the rear areas, but in my platoon, there was no discrimination. I had Black NCOs under me; their men followed them because they were the leaders. Racial strife was rare in the jungle, but the Black Marines left no doubt of their identity. "I'll say it loud, I'm Black and Proud" on a flak jacket was probably against regulations, but I didn't care. We were living in hell's jungle together, and if Joshua and his trumpet were to come by and blow the enemy down, that would have been fine with me.

One of my most striking memories is the night sky. From a three-thousand-foot mountaintop on a moonless night, the stars were huge. There was no light pollution, no noise, no movement—just impenetrable darkness and the stars. I can understand why our ancestors were so taken by the stars. At night they were the whole show. And when the moon was full, it was so bright the stars practically disappeared, and you could write a letter home sitting in front of your hooch.

I remember the unrelenting heat and humidity. I live on the Gulf of Mexico where it is hot and humid during a very long summer. The Gulf Coast is bush league compared to Vietnam, where the heat killed.

I have some souvenirs other than memories—things like photos, an NVA fighting knife, my maps, my rain hat, my John Wayne can opener, crowns on my front teeth and some scars, some medals, and a Chinese SKS rifle I took off a dead NVA for whom I did not feel sorry. The rifle works, but I haven't fired it in years. I have a primitive quiver made from a section of bamboo—about three inches in diameter and a foot long—containing arrows made from hardened wood strips. The "feathers" are made from folded-over leaves, and the points are coated with a hard black material that is supposedly some kind of poison. A small handwoven basket fits over the top. I found it in an abandoned Montagnard village deep in the jungle. One of my men found the crossbow that probably went with it. I would rather have found the bow.

I also have a Chi-com (Chinese communist) grenade. After one firefight, I found it on the ground next to me. Chi-coms were somewhat primitive and unreliable compared to our grenades, but when they went off, they killed just as effectively. Luckily for me, this one had been a dud. I called for the engineers to come blow it in place, but when they got there, the grenade had disappeared. It turned out that one of my Marines had picked it up and disarmed it. He gave it to me later and told me it could have been the end for me, like I wasn't keenly aware of another near miss. I didn't know what to tell him. A Chi-com makes a great souvenir, but you didn't find them lying around since they obviously were made to explode. He could have kept it without anyone knowing. I was touched that had done that for me and told him so. I also told him that fooling with a live grenade could get him killed, or a court-martial if he survived, but I let this one pass and kept the grenade. It's funny how circumstances determine what matters. The grenade sits on the desk in my office.

My girlfriend put the postcard and the Schlitz beer coaster I had mailed to her in a scrapbook, and I still have them. I never told her what combat was really like. Memory of the war was a souvenir I kept to myself. That and my ultimate descent into a beer can had a lot to do with why we're not married anymore.

— 35 —

Friends

People ask me if I have stayed in touch with my buddies from the war. I have not, because I did not make many friends in my war. I made a lot of friends in the Marine Corps; I just didn't make them in Vietnam.

There are three lieutenants, platoon leaders, in a Marine rifle company. We came and went, either by rotation or as casualties, but we were never together long. There wasn't a lot of time for lieutenants to socialize when we were on the move almost every day, so I barely got to know the junior officers I served with. And officers don't become buddies with their men, Big Mike excepted.

The Ninth Marines came ashore at Da Nang in March 1965. Those men knew each other. They had trained together and lived together. There was unit integrity. A Marine's typical stay in a peacetime unit was three years, and where there were shorter tours, there were no casualties to replace. There was plenty of time for a Marine officer to get to know his men. And the men knew who their friends were and whom they could trust.

In wartime, the tour was thirteen months. Marines rotated home or became casualties and had to be replaced. The casualties were just a factor of war, but as time went on, staggered thirteen-month tours put every Marine on a different rotation schedule. After a couple of years, old hands leaving and FNGs arriving was a weekly, sometimes daily event. The result was a complete lack of continuity. Unit integrity suffered. Why the units did not rotate home intact like the Seabees did then, and all units do now, has always been a mystery to me. Sports teams do not win championships by constantly trading off their experienced players without first seasoning their new ones. Somehow nobody figured that out.

The unintended result was that a platoon leader would get to know his squad leaders, and a month later, one would go home. No sooner had his replacement become a part of the platoon command structure when someone else was gone. For the individual troops, it was the same. An FNG would join us, and the men who had been there for a while, and who were in the best position to get him snapped in, would be killed or wounded or rotate home. Most troops didn't form lasting friendships among themselves because the platoon membership was constantly in flux. Men who arrived at about the same time could become buddies if they were in the same squad, but that was determined by chance.

Most critically, there was no opportunity to go back to the rear and relax. They couldn't bullshit, drink, play poker, go whoring in the villages, get in trouble—all the things their fathers and grandfathers did in Europe and the Pacific and

Korea. The statistics show why: the average infantryman in the South Pacific during World War II saw about forty days of combat in four years of service. The average infantryman in Vietnam saw about 240 days of combat in one year. With us, it was always just saddle up and move out.

Very few of the Marine infantry guys I know who fought in the jungle have stayed in touch with the men they fought alongside, because they had such difficulties in getting close, and few of them formed lasting bonds. I have been to a couple of our battalion reunions. All the guys who survived the first year are close because they went in together, and those that survived came out together. The rest are like strangers wandering around the room. They may run into a guy they knew, but since only a small percentage of the men who served in the battalion over the four years it was in country belong to this informal organization, finding a friend is rare. I have run into exactly one of the men who served with me. We suddenly became, and have remained, close.

Other troops, the tankers, cooks, engineers, mechanics, clerks, and other support personnel did not have the same problem. They did not suffer the same rate of casualties, and they spent much of their time in rear areas. They could play poker and go whoring in the villages. In the helicopter-mobile infantry, we never caught our breath. I believe the forced impersonality of infantry combat contributed to the overall sense of aloneness that many Vietnam veterans still feel.

—36—

Home

They told us not to react to anything we might hear in the Los Angeles airport when we came home. It was October 1969. The people did not stand and applaud us like they often do for our modern warriors. As we walked down the concourse after deplaning, a couple of hippies spit in our direction and called us baby killers. I often think that if I had been armed, I would have rid the world of two hippies. We had lived through a hell they could not begin to imagine. We didn't expect a parade, but we didn't expect to be spit at either. If you ever hear two old guys saying, "Welcome home, brother," you'll know why. It is not a joke. It was hard to come home from what we had been through when our countrymen at best ignored us and at worst despised us.

Vietnam veterans became national lepers. Some small part of it was deserved. Isolated atrocities like the massacre at My Lai happened. Villages were burned down. Civilians did die. But part of our humiliation was indirectly self-imposed by phonies coming home and making themselves killer heroes:

"I was with fuckin' X-Ray Force in The 'Nam, man. Don't ever startle me when I'm fuckin' sleeping 'cause I might cut your fuckin' throat before I wake up."

It was all crap, but with time the image of psychopaths who burned down villages and raped and murdered innocents came to include all of us. "He's one of them crazy Veet Nam veterans just as soon kill ya as look at ya." I heard that more than once. The war had supposedly so brutalized us that we were dangerous and not to be trusted. Pitied, maybe, but not trusted. Then at some point after the war was over, Vietnam veterans became invisible, our service and sacrifice ignored unless one of us generated a headline like "Crazed Vietnam Veteran Kills Wife, Self." If the killer was a Marine, the story ran for a week. Apparently, vets of earlier wars never did anything newsworthy unless it involved pulling someone from a burning building.

But for us, there was always an underlying suspicion, a distance, even though most of us went to work and tried to get on with our lives. Friends would wonder, but wouldn't ask, if you had burned down a village or killed civilians. You could see it in their faces. They inquired obliquely by asking if you wanted to talk about the war like they were doing you the favor of offering personal therapy. That was all crap too. For a long time, I didn't care what anyone thought, and I was not anxious to revisit buried memories.

After the 1991 Gulf War, which lasted on the ground for all of four days, soldiers became heroes because we won. Returning troops paraded until they were sick of it. Vietnam veterans had no parades but finally became acceptable curiosities. We were getting old; we were homeless men in ragged uniforms, begging at street corners. People expressed surprise that those of us who led outwardly normal lives—and take my word for it, we are the huge majority—had been in the war. If pressed, we might tell them a happy memory, like the story about the Seabee bar. That always got a laugh. We don't tell stories like the one about the boots or the kid in the hole or the death of Big Mike or the monstrous brutality of it all. And we don't tell of the aftermath in our own lives. We put on a good face and shrugged it off. Today, although embroiled in another unpopular war, the aftermath of a war we thought had been won, we all "support our troops," even when as individuals, some of them do evil. In the 1970s and after, our national conscience was assuaged by transferring the evil done by those few who committed crimes in Vietnam to the nearly two million young men who did not commit crimes, for no reason other than to ease the lingering anguish brought on by the decision to go to war in the first place.

The tragedy of this war is not measured only in wounds and the loss of lives. There is psychological injury too. We were fighting to the death in a war that the country had largely turned against, and we could look for support only from our families and fellow Marines. The men also suspected, although they never said, that the whole thing was a waste. We knew we could win. If we could go after the enemy in their sanctuaries, we could force an end to the communists' aggression; we also understood somehow that we would not be allowed to win. My guys were being cheated, and all too many paid the ultimate price for the nation's decision to go to war and later show a complete lack of the resolve necessary to finish it.

Watching Ken Burns's *The Vietnam War* taught me something I had long suspected but couldn't prove: our national leadership actively sacrificed us. Call it pride, call it greed, call it power, call it what you want, but in the end, it was cowardice. Assuming Burns's research was accurate, President Truman secretly sent transport planes to South Vietnam. President Kennedy was quoted as saying, "There are only so many sacrifices we can make and still survive politically." That was in 1961 when Kennedy was sending advisers and war materiel to South Vietnam while lying about the buildup. In the spring of 1963, Kennedy was reported as saying, "We don't have a prayer of staying in Vietnam. These people hate us. But I can't give up a piece of territory like that to the communists and then get the people to reelect me." Later that year President Johnson said he knew Vietnam was not worth fighting for, saying, "We haven't got a Congress that'll go with us and we haven't got any mothers that will go with us in the war, and I got to win an election and then make a decision [about getting out]." Johnson continued to commit troops while knowing no end was in sight.

Richard Nixon, running for president in 1968, said: "I've concluded that there's no way to win this war, but we have to say the opposite just to keep some bargaining leverage [in peace talks]." And as president in March 1971: "I have become completely fatalistic about the goddamn thing. We're going to get the hell out and hope nothing happens before 1972 [and the next election]. Let's face it. If my reelection is important, I've got to get this off my plate." And finally, also in 1971, four years before all American troops were pulled out of Vietnam: "South Vietnam will never survive, but we have to win an election."

These men, the elected elite of our nation, were so afraid of looking like they were "soft on communism," and, excepting Truman and Eisenhower, who were not looking at being reelected, were so keen on getting elected or reelected while knowing the war was a loser, allowed the war to continue, willingly sacrificing the lives of American troops. They sent young men to die so they could stay in office. They murdered Americans. It was abominable. I cannot think of a more monstrous crime.

— 37 —

After

I have long since recovered from my physical wounds, but like many of my brothers, physical recovery is not the end. Over the many years since coming home, I have thought a lot about the war, mostly trying to make sense of it and of my part in it, and whether we did anything there besides bring untold grief to two nations. The decade of the '60s was a confused time in our country. Everywhere there was tumult, from a Free Speech Movement student walking across the campus at Berkeley, provoking The Establishment by carrying a sign reading only "FUCK," to the long-haired Beatles, Freedom Riders, the assassination of John Kennedy, Woodstock, the drug overdose death of Janis Joplin, American soldiers killing American students at Kent State, the marches on Washington, dogs and fire hoses in Birmingham, LSD, pot, violence at Selma, Jane Fonda in Hanoi calling us murderers, John Kerry before congress calling us murderers and rapists, Bob Dylan "Blowin' in the Wind," Dr. King's riveting dream, the Pentagon Papers, President Johnson's decision not to run for another term, the Summer of Love in San Francisco, the assassinations of Dr. King and Bobby Kennedy, self-immolations in front of the Pentagon—the list goes on. Much of the unrest came from the civil rights movement, but much was driven by the war.

In 1966, in the middle of all that chaos, I was a year from finishing college. A shooting war was going on, and I thought our nation had an opportunity and an obligation to stop the march of communism, so I volunteered. In 1966 the country generally favored getting into the fight. I was draft-eligible, and getting drafted was not an attractive option, so I looked for the fastest way to a commission. Marine Corps OCS was the only viable choice, and although it was fast, it was far from easy.

The national mood had changed radically by the time I came home. It seemed that I and many others had done our part for an ungrateful nation, and so received our due, which was very little. The government that sent us to war later denied that those of us who survived had suffered any real damage. At times, the politicians joined the popular chorus in blaming us for our supposedly imagined postwar wounds. The sense of betrayal felt by so many veterans has been profound. I think we lost the war and lost our national soul at the same time, because the policymakers wasted so many lives in the forlorn hope that everything would work out and that they would be reelected, then lacked the guts to get out when things went south. And somehow it became accepted dogma that the men who fought the war were at fault.

Finally, veterans convinced the Congress to authorize a Vietnam Memorial and then paid for it themselves.

Veterans forced the government to look at Agent Orange and posttraumatic stress disorder. Veterans created the POW/MIA flag and then shamed the government into searching for the remains of their missing brothers, a search that still goes on at the cost of millions. And while we search for American remains, a Vietnamese kid is buried in a hole somewhere in the jungle who will never be found. He will never be looked for, and he is just one of thousands.

— 38 —

Long After

Life went on. I went back to school. The GI Bill (provided, I admit, by a not entirely ungrateful nation), my savings from my time in Vietnam, a stint in the active reserves with a Marine Reserve motor transport company, plus two part-time jobs and a working wife helped me earn a law degree from the University of Florida at Gainesville. I had been encouraged to go to law school by a Marine lawyer while I was convalescing in Okinawa. He regaled me nightly at the Officers Club bar and urged me to try the law. He was base defense counsel and had a good track record of getting the guilty set free, at least that's how I saw it. His success offended my sense of right and wrong, but that was his job, and he was good at it and enjoyed it. He continued to encourage me to become a lawyer, and I owe him a lot for his persistence.

Law school was not your usual postgrad experience. I never felt like a student. Going to law school was an intellectual challenge but a sterile one. I went to school in the morning and went home at night. School spirit was not part of my life. I never went to a football game and do not consider myself a Gator. I didn't get the sense I was being trained for anything because I knew about training. They didn't teach us how to get to the courthouse, much less what to do when we got there. It was all theory, no reality. Then they turned us loose on an unsuspecting public.

My class contained ten Vietnam veterans. We were three or four years older than our classmates, but a great emotional chasm existed between us. The others were children. We did not relate. I can't say they shunned us, but no one appreciated anything we had done. To our classmates, we were fools for having gone to war. Many of my classmates—almost all were men in those days—have gone on to become hotshot lawyers, but their war stories are confined to the courtroom. They may think they have been to war, but in comparison to those few of us who were willing to stand up and be counted when standing up was a likely death sentence, they have lived the ultimate soft lives. Rich and self-satisfied as many of them are, I don't envy them. They have never lived because they have never almost died.

Antiwar demonstrations were held in the streets of Gainesville in the early 1970s, some of which turned violent, but I ignored them. I didn't support the war. I didn't protest the war. I didn't care. I had lost the desire to care, all the while knowing that the war was still going on, and young men were dying every day while the government sought "Peace with Honor." As I said, it was criminal. By this time what national honor we had left was not worth the life of a single man, but thousands more died, and more treasure was squandered. At the same time, we endured the humiliation of negotiating an end to our participation in Vietnam, finally accepting North Vietnamese promises we knew they would not keep while promising the South Vietnamese support we would ultimately withhold.

I graduated in 1973 and was hired by a good law firm run by an old World War II Marine in Pensacola, Florida. He hired me based largely on my combat history. Marines are like that. He was a wonderful boss, and I miss him. I tried to stay in the active reserves, but by then, infantry captains were a dime a dozen, and the local tank and recon reserve units didn't have slots for me. In 1976, without forewarning or fanfare, I received an honorable discharge in the mail.

In the meantime, I had turned to a different kind of warfare. I became a civil trial lawyer. I was a good one and was fearless in the courtroom. Trial practice is an adversarial process. It is like war without the blood. It is single combat. I fought as champion for my client; opposing counsel fought as champion for theirs. In any case, an intelligent, motivated, and trained opponent was always trying to undo whatever I did, to defeat my strategy, to beat my client, to win the battle. I thrived on that battlefield. My job was not to kill but to sell a point of view to a jury, and I had more than my share of victories. I was doing something that had meaning for the litigants, something that would be appreciated by my clients, and something that mattered.

As I gained experience and reputation, I became a partner in the firm. National and international clients kept me on the go. That meant my services were needed in other places, which required flying off to some destination to try a case or take a deposition. I despised flying. I had nightmares about falling and burning, and getting on an airplane was unsettling, no matter how many times I did it. In 1985, I withdrew from the law firm to open a solo practice that would hopefully keep me at home. In 1996, I quit trying cases. I don't fly anymore if I can avoid it.

Years after I quit trying cases, a good friend—a former opponent in the courtroom—told me that during my trial career, my opponents referred to me as "The Slasher," because I would often slash their cases to shreds. Maybe I did. I like the name, though. Being a slasher is better than being a butcher, particularly when nobody dies. And unlike in real combat, opposing counsel very often became friends. That was really the best part—camaraderie with the enemy.

Away from work, I stayed quiet. My contemporaries were interested in happy hour, in partying, and in having fun. I was interested in staying sane. I felt like I had used up an entire lifetime in less than a year, something others could never begin to understand, and I felt old. I could see a future out there, but I couldn't see how I was going to fit in it. I always felt that I was on the outside looking in. I don't think I was bitter, but in the quiet of my soul, I couldn't escape the feeling that I had simply been used up and thrown away in the jungle. I had done nothing wrong, had committed no crimes, had led my Marines effectively, and had served and was ultimately discharged honorably, but the gnawing feeling of guilt or remorse or aloneness or some great intangible nothingness would not go away.

My family suffered without understanding why. I drank more and more, and although I kept my job and was successful in it, I increasingly found no joy in much of anything but alcohol. I drank at home and stayed out of trouble, so nobody but my suffering family could see my slow slide into insanity.

After a while, even the alcohol let me down. It could no longer erase the anxieties or the memories or the emptiness that were trying to consume me. In October 1989, coincidentally twenty years almost to the day after arriving in Los Angeles to be spit at, I finally accepted the fact that I was facing true insanity or prison or suicide and quit drinking. There were still demons about, but at least I could begin to deal with them without the fog of drunkenness. As I write this, I have not taken a drink in more then thirty years. Sobriety has been its own reward. A treatment center and Alcoholics Anonymous saved my life.

I resisted going to the VA for medical care until ten or twelve years ago, and then went only after I ran into one of my Kilo Marines at a reunion, a veterans' representative in Illinois who convinced me that help was available. I didn't trust the VA. Like many other Vietnam vets, I looked at the VA as, while not the enemy, not a friend. It represented the government—the one we had fought for that later blamed us and then ignored us. Worse, during the Agent Orange controversy after the war, the VA claimed to be the primary spokesman for the veteran while simultaneously telling its own physicians that the chances of physical damage being caused by herbicide exposure were virtually zero. It was a lie then, and they knew it. The VA claimed it was our representative during those early years, but it was working hard against us. The VA didn't want to address the Agent Orange issue for political reasons. There was insufficient money, and manufacturers of the chemicals put pressure on the Congress and the president.

What really hurt was that supposedly patriotic groups like the American Legion and the VFW were dismissing the whole conversation as coming from a bunch of crybaby losers.

I don't belong to any such organizations, nor will I ever. And I believe that the VA came to harbor an institutional dislike for Vietnam veterans. It turned its back on us. In any event, I was a Marine. Admitting defeat by alcohol was bad enough. Admitting emotional defeat was something else. I didn't want to go to a VA psychologist.

So, the VA psychologist told me, big surprise, that my combat history, wounds and injuries, alcoholism, depression, and two divorces supported a finding that I was an alcoholic in remission with clinical depression and PTSD. At least I wasn't crazy. I knew I was an alcoholic and depressed, but by then, I had been sober for many years and was being successfully treated for depression. I haven't decided whether the PTSD diagnosis made me feel better or worse.

The VA's treatment plan for PTSD was a weekly two-hour group session at noon. I went for a while. It was difficult because I had a full-time job without the luxury of a two-hour lunch break. I quit going after a couple of weeks when I realized that although the dozen or so other guys in the group were all Vietnam vets, they were all REMFs—rear echelon motherfuckers—with no combat arms experience or Purple Heart in the bunch. I respected their service because we could not have survived in the jungle without them, and surely they had legitimate reasons for being in treatment, but I could not relate to their terrors. Or maybe it was my ego. After all, I had been a Marine rifle platoon leader, and not many people can say that. Based on the number of rifle platoons in the two Marine divisions that fought in Vietnam, if my math is correct, there were barely more than two hundred young men doing what I was doing at any one time. The Marines' war lasted just over four years. If platoon leaders changed every four months, there were roughly twenty-five hundred Marines (out of three hundred million Americans) who did what I did, and many of them have their names inscribed on the Wall. Okay, it was my ego. The other guys in the PTSD class were just whiners. I know. Unfair.

The psychologist suggested I write down some of the events that haunted me, so that's what this is. Writing it has been depressing and liberating at the same time. War is a nasty business, and for me, it hasn't entirely gone away. I spent almost eight months in a war in which death was a daily, hourly presence. We beat the enemy at every turn, but no end was in sight, and we sensed it. We also sensed that our sacrifice would end up being pointless because of our country's refusal to do what it would take to win. I now realize that it is dehumanizing to go through what we went through knowing, then as now, that nobody would ever give a damn. So, I got in the bottle and was a little screwed up. Now I'm okay, life is good, and sometimes people do seem to give a damn.

I like to say I have survived damn near everything and have a little sign on the wall of my office that says so. Fifty-eight thousand young Americans did not survive, all because our political leaders knew nothing about fighting a guerilla war, and then didn't know how to finish what they had started, or more accurately, were too cowardly to admit their mistakes. Everybody knows we lost the war. The military blames it on the politicians. The politicians blame it on the military. Long after the war was over, former Secretary of Defense McNamara wrote a book where he tentatively accepted responsibility while blaming the loss on everyone but himself. Whether the war was winnable I can't say. If we had been allowed to attack and disrupt the Ho Chi Minh trail in Laos and Cambodia, perhaps. I think the real legacy of the Vietnam War is the endless national tragedy of sweeping it all under the rug and wishing it away.

— 39 —

Return

I returned to Vietnam in 1999 with a tour group of old Marines. For reasons I still don't understand, I wanted to see the Dewey Canyon operation area, to revisit the place where my life had been so irrevocably altered, where so many lives on both sides had been taken, and where I had lost Mike.

We flew from Hong Kong to Hanoi, which was dirty and smelled overwhelmingly of mildew. Most of the streets were paved, but dust was everywhere. I was amused to find a small monument next to a lake near the center of town. It memorialized the heroic people of Hanoi who swam out to rescue a pilot named John McCain after he parachuted into the lake and would have drowned but for the heroic actions of the people. The monument appeared to be relatively new. I'm sure it was not erected while Lieutenant Commander John McCain was being tortured in the nearby Hanoi Hilton.

We did get a tour of the infamous prison. They told us the captured Americans had it pretty easy there, and the

Vietnamese considered it a privilege to have been their guardians. None of this gave me a positive feeling. We saw the Ho Chi Minh mausoleum with Uncle Ho preserved under glass. He still looked rather good for a guy who had been dead for thirty years. He enjoys a true cult following in the country, and the mausoleum was crowded with locals.

We also went to a military museum in Hanoi. My war was variously described there as the American War, the Imperialist American Criminal War, the United States Aggression War, and the American War to Prevent Reunification. The museum tour was not a happy one for me. Certainly, the winners write the history, but coming face-to-face with how they defeated the criminal running dog capitalist Americans and reading that "heroic combatant" so-and-so used this particular AK-47 to kill twenty-seven of the imperialist murderers was not pleasant. It was probably true, and we would have written a similar history had we won, so I couldn't complain too much. Still, I could not let go of all the good Marines I saw die. I still felt angry. I couldn't forget Mike. But good men on both sides died, and for what? Communist Vietnam is now a trading partner with the United States. We buy their wares at Wal-Mart, cheap. One of my USMC ballcaps was made in Vietnam.

Aside from the isolated war propaganda, the Vietnamese people were unfailingly friendly. Everyone had something to sell, and they all tried to communicate in English, which surprised me. There were happy smiles everywhere. I sensed that the people were glad to see us, and not just for our tourist money. This was unexpected given our recent history with these people, but none of that history seemed to matter. Vietnamese children were being taught English as their second language. We couldn't go anywhere without hearing kids shout "Hello!" at the tops of their voices. The nation's official currency was the dong, but the US dollar was accepted by merchants in even the most far-flung village, where everyone seemed to know the current exchange rate to the penny.

I did learn a few things about enlightened communism while I was there. In 1988, Cuban engineers had paved Route 14, the Ho Chi Minh Highway, which runs north and south up the center of the country. It was once a footpath over which I trod many times. As part of the project, they built a large suspension bridge over the Da Krong River just east of Khe Sanh. I estimate that the bridge spanned about a quarter of a mile. I couldn't tell how long any particular span was, or how many piers there were because in 1997 the bridge fell into the river. On the north side, I saw the butt ends of many huge cables, but that was about all. Google Earth shows a rebuilt bridge.

One night we stayed at a three-story hotel in Dong Ha. It had been built by the Russians. Standing by the front wall and looking up was disquieting, because the entire wall bulged out what looked like a good three feet. I thought the building was about to fall over. One nervous night was enough to convince me that this would never be a tourist destination. I'm not saying Cuban and Russian engineers were at fault. I'm just reporting what I saw.

After spending a night at the leaning hotel of Dong Ha, we took four-wheelers west on Route 9, still a dirt road, passed by the Rockpile, and stopped at VCB. There was no sign that we were ever there. A village occupied the site, but I could see no recognizable landmark. Farther west on Route 9 brought us to Khe Sanh. During the war, Khe Sanh was a combat base with an airstrip. Now it is a bustling town. The old base is planted in coffee, but nothing seems to grow on the airstrip itself. What was once the control tower has become a museum celebrating the peoples' victory over the American aggressors. The building was not air-conditioned, and what war souvenirs were there were either rusting or crumbling away, as was the building, which I'm told has since been rebuilt.

From Khe Sanh looking north I could see Hill 950—the jungle-covered hilltop that had once been Third Platoon's little place of respite—and I could see no evidence that there had ever been an observation post there. The jungle has reclaimed it.

Heading back east, we stopped to look down the mountainside at a village of Bru tribesmen, some of the Montagnards that were resettled to the coast during the war. They were back home in the mountains, tending their banana trees and cornfields. Their village was perhaps the most picturesque place I have ever seen.

Part of the tour was to a series of tunnels just north of the old DMZ, where the people hid when the B-52s came. It was near the sea, and I had time to walk down and watch fishermen pulling their nets onto the beach. They were poor but very friendly and took me over to see a large horseshoe crab they had caught. We could not communicate effectively, but interacting with these people was one of the highlights of my trip. Somehow the long-buried anger and resentments seemed momentarily to fade. These were just people going about their everyday lives, and they seemed happy. I thought what a shame it is that politicians periodically ruin things for us. Later we stopped at a cemetery of heroes killed by the

American aggressors. It was overgrown with weeds, and the stone markers had already started to crumble. I thought about the kid in the hole.

We went into the mountains in four-wheelers on dirt trails. Route 14, once a dirt trail, then paved but now more a dirt road than a highway, went right through the heart of the Dewey Canyon operation area. When we got there, I got out of my vehicle, and I was back. The smells and the memories were in the jungle all around me, and for good or evil, the jungle was still the jungle. I walked off the road for about fifty yards, just to get the feel. I saw and felt the small stream running by my feet, the vines entwined among monstrous trees, the odor of rotting vegetation, the overwhelming presence of green, the brooding enormity of the place where I still couldn't see anything but the jungle in front of me. It all came back. The sense of being exactly where I had been so many years before was riveting. There was a difference, though. I could hear animal noises—birds singing, small animals scurrying through the leaves, hoots, and caws—sounds I had never heard in this place before. Somehow that gave me the feeling that the world was different, was better, that nature had ultimately triumphed, as it always does. I can't say the experience was cathartic. I can't say it was not. I can't say what it was.

Suddenly I thought maybe the jungle wasn't so alive. It didn't feel right. In some sense, I felt as if I had just been reborn, dumped ignorant and innocent into a surreal place yet cursed with memories from an earlier life. The memories would not go away. Big Mike was there. Preacher and the kid and others were there. There was life in the jungle, but death somehow hovered nearby. I knew I couldn't stay. We got back in the four-wheelers and bumped our way back to the coast.

– 40 –

It Is Over

I am glad I made the trip. It had its haunting moments, but it reinforced my belief in human resiliency. People in power can do as they will, but the human drive to survive and prosper will not be destroyed. These people, who had been my most hated enemies, were now just people, fishing, farming, building houses, and riding their bicycles, living out their days without obvious help or hindrance from their communist rulers. No doubt under a democratic government such as ours they would be more free, but they were not outwardly enslaved. Stalin's gulag, if it existed in Vietnam, was well hidden. Millions of southerners died or were placed in re-education camps after the 1975 northern victory, but the people now have largely forgotten that ugly part of their past. Life expectancy in this third world country is still only about sixty years, so even the old people barely remember the American war. As I said earlier, they are learning English, and they sell us their products. Vietnam is a net exporter of rice to the rest of Asia. It is wealthy compared to many of its neighbors.

While touring Marble Mountain, a favorite tourist spot on the coast, I met a young couple from Colorado. He was obviously Anglo, and she was obviously Vietnamese, but she had been born in America and spoke only English. They were on a tour of her ancestral homeland, which was totally foreign to her. It gave me a strange feeling like the world was somehow out of joint, but it made perfect sense for these two young people to be tourists just like I was.

Although there is still a great deal of deserved bitterness among American Vietnam veterans, the Vietnamese seem to have put the war behind them. What I have concluded may not be well accepted among my brothers, given the deaths, destruction, and waste of national treasure on both sides, but I honestly believe that if we had never intervened in Vietnam, our two countries would be exactly as they are now, except that those who died there would be grandparents, and those of us who survived would have lived emotionally easier lives.

In 1965 our philosophical fight was against the communists. Communism was a disease that the Russians and Chinese were trying to spread worldwide. It was also a system of freedom denied, secret police, mass graves, oppression, and government control of every facet of peoples' lives. But the Soviet Union is dead, and although China is still communist, it is working to beat us economically as well as politically. I haven't seen any recent signs that international communism is a philosophy trying to export itself worldwide. And as to the murders, loss of freedom and oppression, I vividly recall that we as a nation supported a lot of right-wing tin-pot dictators over the years, from Francisco Franco to Augusto Pinochet to the apartheid regime of South Africa, solely because they were anticommunist. Still, I do not recall that they gave their people a lot of freedom. Their secret police were everywhere, as were their mass graves. My point is that communism and military dictatorships are bad systems, but the dictatorships are homegrown and not exportable. And we have a different enemy now. So, if we had never gone to war there, Vietnam would be communist as it is now, the Soviet Union would still have collapsed, and China would be an economic threat. Perhaps if all our angry vets went back as I did, they would feel a little differently about our former enemies. Now looking back, I can see that for me, the trip was therapeutic.

We had a host assigned to us, a young man from some government agency in Hanoi. He said his name was Trahn. He was faultlessly polite, spoke excellent English, and laughed when we told him we knew he was from the Vietnamese KGB. Near the end of our tour, one of our group asked Trahn why the people were so accepting of Americans when the war had done so much damage and had taken so many lives.

"The Vietnamese people," Trahn said, "were dominated by the Chinese for a thousand years and by the French for a hundred years, but we are not a people who look back. The American War was something that happened, but it is over."

Printed in the United States
by Baker & Taylor Publisher Services